Kitchen
Comforts

Recipes to Feed Body and Soul

Gay T. Boassy

Simple Dream

Original Artwork and Recipes © Gay T. Boassy, licensed by Leo Licensing, LLC, Cookeville, TN

Editor: Angela Rahaniotis

© 2005 Simple Dream Publishing Inc.
info@simpledream.ca

ISBN 1-897115-07-5

Printed in China

In a household of ten (my husband, eight kids and myself) if you don't want trouble, you better have plenty of food available. And when seven of those ten people are boys, and big boys at that, it is much more difficult than one might think.

When my children were young, I began cooking dinner at around three in the afternoon in order to have it ready in time for six or seven o'clock in the evening. And everything was on a grand scale, at least in terms of quantity. Sometimes that meant doubling or tripling a recipe. It also meant that, like with so many families, dinner was sometimes squeezed in between football or baseball practice. All told, over the last twenty years I have spent a whole lot of time in the kitchen and at the ball park. But even with all the chaos, many of our best times were spent around the dinner table.

I am not a chef, but I am a cook. I admit that I have been known to measure my flour or sugar with a coffee cup, and a teaspoon of seasoning with a teaspoon from the drawer, if I measure at all. Still, it seems to work out just fine. I have a beautiful set of measuring cups. They are a perfect shade of robin's egg blue and nest inside each other. But I just can't bring myself to use them because they are much too pretty to risk breaking. So, I keep them under a glass dome on the center of the island in my kitchen. I suppose it pleases me more just seeing them there on center stage.

The truth of the matter is, more often than not, I cook simply by how it "looks". So if it looks like enough sugar, great, or if it looks like it needs a bit more, I go ahead and put it in. It is all about feeling comfortable with a recipe, and adapting it to make it your own. My theory on cooking is this: If you think it would taste better with less of one thing, or by adding something that is not in the recipe, or by leaving out something you don't particularly care for: go right ahead. You can always try it differently the next time if you don't like it.

Be bold, take a chance, be creative, and above all, relax. After all, food is meant to be a comfort, not something to get stressed over!

Contents

When I was young, my mother often entertained her friends from the church we attended. And she always set out plenty of choices on her table to make sure everyone had something they liked. Isn't it always a good idea to give your guests, and your family, lots of great choices? I have tried to provide a variety of "little bites" here for entertaining or for starting off a great meal.

Although getting an appetite started has never been a problem at our house, there are many occasions when these little bites come in handy. At my home, it generally means making three or four times the recipe yield to accommodate my children and their friends.

Some of our favorites are: Oyster Cracker Snack, Queso Dip with Cornbread and Pigs in a Blanket. My kids call them "Hogs in a Quilt". Oh well, a snack by any other name still tastes as good.

Appetizers

SPICY CRAB DEVILED EGGS

8 hard-boiled eggs
1/4 cup mayonnaise or salad dressing
1 tbsp finely chopped green onion
1 to 2 tsp flavored mustard, such as Dijon-style or horseradish
1/4 tsp salt
1/4 tsp cayenne pepper
1 to 2 tbsp mango chutney
3 tbsp mayonnaise or salad dressing
1/2 tsp curry powder
1/2 cup cooked crabmeat (about 2 3/4 ounces)

Halve the hard-boiled eggs lengthwise and remove yolks.
Set whites aside.
In a quart-size, self-sealing plastic bag place egg yolks,
the 1/4-cup mayonnaise, the green onion, mustard,
1/8 teaspoon of the salt, and 1/8 teaspoon of the cayenne pepper.
Seal bag. Gently squeeze the bag to combine ingredients.
Snip one corner of the bag and pipe mixture into egg white
halves. Cut up any large pieces of chutney. In a bowl, combine
the chutney, the 3 tablespoons mayonnaise, curry powder,
remaining 1/8-teaspoon salt, and remaining 1/8-teaspoon cayenne
pepper. Gently fold in crabmeat.
Make each deviled egg with a spoonful of the crab mixture.
Cover and chill for 1 to 2 hours.

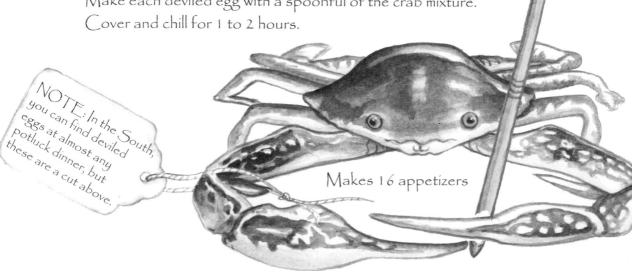

NOTE: In the South,
you can find deviled
eggs at almost any
potluck dinner, but
these are a cut above.

Makes 16 appetizers

ROMANO SHRIMP-STUFFED MUSHROOMS

20 large fresh mushrooms
5 oz. small cooked shrimp, rinsed, drained and chopped
1 carton soft cream cheese with chives
1/2 tsp Worcestershire sauce
Dash of garlic powder
2 to 3 drops of hot sauce
1/4 cup grated Romano cheese

Clean mushrooms with damp paper towels. Remove stems
and reserve for later use. Set caps aside.
Combine all remaining ingredients, except Romano cheese. Mix well.
Spoon mixture into mushroom caps and sprinkle with cheese.
Place mushrooms in a lightly greased 11x7x2-inch baking pan.
Cover and chill 2 to 3 hours.
Uncover and bake at 400° F for 14 minutes.

Makes 20 appetizers

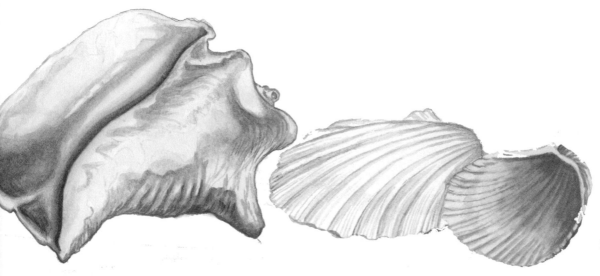

HAM and GOUDA QUESADILLAS

2 8-9 inch flour tortillas
1 cup shredded Gouda or smoked mozzarella cheese
1/2 cup chopped smoked ham
2 tbsp snipped fresh parsley
1/4 cup dairy sour cream
Parsley sprigs

Sprinkle cheese over half of each tortilla.
Top with ham and parsley.
Fold tortillas in half, pressing gently.
In a lightly greased 10-inch skillet or griddle,
cook quesadillas over medium heat for 2 to 3 minutes
or until lightly browned, turning once.
Cut quesadillas into wedges. Serve with sour cream.
Garnish with parsley sprigs if you like.

Makes 2 full size servings, or may be cut into triangles for
8 appetizers

CHEESE and OLIVE BALLS

2 cups grated sharp
 cheese
1/2 cup butter, softened
1 cup sifted flour
1 tsp paprika

Dash of cayenne pepper
1/2 tsp salt
50 pitted green olives

Blend cheese with softened butter.
Stir in flour and seasonings, which have been sifted together.
Mix well.
Wrap 1 tsp cheese mixture around each olive, covering it completely.
Arrange on a baking sheet and chill or freeze until firm.
Bake at 400° F for 15 minutes. Serve hot.

Makes 50 appetizers

PIGS in a BLANKET
a.k.a.: Hogs in a Quilt

8-oz. tube refrigerated crescent rolls
12oz. smoked sausage links

Separate the dough into eight triangles.
Place a sausage on wide end of each triangle and roll up.
Place, tip down, on an ungreased baking sheet.
Bake at 400° F for 10-15 minutes or until golden brown.

Makes 8 appetizers

PINEAPPLE CHEESE BALL

2 8-oz. pkg. cream cheese softened (I use fat-free)
2 tbsp finely chopped bell pepper
2 tbsp finely chopped onion
1/4 cup drained crushed pineapple
2 tsp seasoned salt
2 cups chopped pecans, divided
Fresh strawberries, or raspberries, mint or pineapple
 chunks for garnish

In a medium size bowl, beat cream cheese until
smooth.
Add bell pepper, onion, pineapple, seasoned salt
and 1 cup of the pecans. Mix well.
Shape into 2 small or 1 large ball and roll in
remainder of pecans.
Chill before serving and decorate with fresh fruit.
Serve with decorative crackers.

Serves 10

PARTY MEATBALLS

1 lb. ground beef
1 egg, slightly beaten
1/2 cup bread crumbs
1/4 cup milk
1 tsp salt
1/4 tsp pepper
1 small onion, minced
1 tbsp Worcestershire sauce
1/2 tsp garlic salt
1 large (32-oz.) jar of grape jelly
1 large bottle of chili sauce

In a large bowl, mix all ingredients together until blended. Roll into small balls, about 1 1/2 inches in diameter. Place on a cookie sheet and bake in 350º F oven for 15 minutes.
In a saucepan, melt jelly and chili sauce.
Add meatballs to sauce.
Keep warm until ready to serve. Serve with toothpicks.

Makes approximately 30 meatballs

NOTE: A good way to serve these warm is to keep them in a small crock-pot on low.

FRIED GREEN TOMATOES

1 cup cornmeal
1 tbsp flour
Salt and pepper to taste
4 or so green tomatoes, sliced
Vegetable oil (start with 1/8 cup, you may want to add more)
1/2 cup grated Parmesan cheese

Mix together cornmeal, flour, salt and pepper.
Wash and slice the tomatoes.
Dip tomato slices in the cornmeal mixture.
Fry in medium skillet with vegetable oil until golden brown on both sides.
Sprinkle with Parmesan cheese immediately upon removing from pan.

Makes approximately 4 to 6 servings

NOTE: These make a great appetizer or salad sprinkled with feta cheese on top and drizzled with Ranch dressing. They also make a wonderful sandwich on toasted bread with sliced smoked Gouda cheese and Thousand Island dressing spread on the bread.

to-MA-to
tom-A-to

CRESCENT MARSHMALLOW PUFFS

1/4 cup sugar
1 tsp cinnamon
2 8-oz. cans Pillsbury Crescent Dinner rolls
16 marshmallows (large)
1/4 cup butter or margarine (melted)
1/4 cup nuts (chopped, optional)

GLAZE
1/2 cup powdered sugar
1/2 tsp vanilla
2-3 tsp milk

Combine sugar with cinnamon.
Separate crescent dough into 16 triangles.
Dip a marshmallow in melted butter; roll in sugar and
cinnamon mixture.
Wrap a dough triangle around each marshmallow,
completely covering marshmallow and squeeze edges of
dough tightly to seal.
Dip in melted butter and place buttered-side down in deep
muffin cups.
Repeat with remaining marshmallows. Place pan on layer of
foil in case of spill over.
Bake at 375° F for 10-15 minutes until golden brown.
In a small bowl, mix glaze ingredients.
Drizzle over puffs before serving.

Makes 16 puffs

CHEESE WAFERS

8 oz. sharp cheese, grated
1 cup flour
1 stick (1/2 cup) margarine
2 cups rice cereal
1/4 tsp red pepper
1/2 tsp salt

Mix all ingredients. Shape into small balls. Place on a lightly greased baking sheet and flatten with a fork. Bake at 300° F until brown around edges.

Makes about 40 wafers

OYSTER CRACKER SNACK

16-oz. box oyster crackers
1/4 cup vegetable oil
1-oz. packet Hidden Valley Ranch Dressing Mix

Place crackers in a large plastic bag. Pour oil over crackers and toss to coat. Add dressing mix; toss again until coated.
Place on a cookie sheet with sides.
Bake at 250° F for 15 to 20 minutes. Let cool before serving.

Makes about 3 cups

FETA CHEESE APPETIZERS

1 small onion, finely chopped (1/3 cup)
3 cloves garlic, minced
2 tsp olive oil or cooking oil
8-oz. pkg. cream cheese
4 oz. crumbled feta cheese
1/2 cup chopped pitted Kalamata olives
1/4 cup chopped roasted sweet
 red peppers
1 tsp dried dill weed
3 pita bread rounds

NOTE: I leave out the olives, my personal taste, and I use fat-free feta and cream cheeses.

Preheat broiler. In a medium skillet, cook onion and garlic in olive oil over medium heat for 4 to 5 minutes, or until onion is tender. Remove from heat. Add cream cheese and feta cheese; stir until mixture is nearly smooth.
Stir in olives, sweet peppers and dill weed. Set aside.
Using a long serrated knife, split pita rounds in half horizontally to form two circles. Place cut side up, on a large ungreased baking sheet. Broil 3 inches from heat for 1 minute or until pita rounds are lightly toasted.
Spread each pita round with about 1/3 cup of the cheese mixture. Broil about 1 minute more, or until hot.
To serve, use a sharp knife to cut each circle into 8 wedges.

Makes 24 appetizers

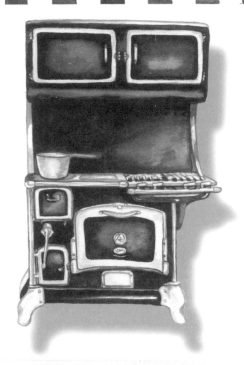

QUESO DIP with CORNBREAD

8 1/2- oz. pkg. corn muffin mix (I like Jiffy brand.)
2 fresh poblano chile peppers
1 small sweet red pepper
3 cups shredded Monterey Jack cheese
2 tbsp all-purpose flour
1/3 cup finely chopped onion
1 tbsp butter or margarine
3/4 cup half-and-half (I use fat-free)
1/3 cup finely chopped, peeled jicama

CORNBREAD

For the cornbread, prepare corn muffin mix according to package directions.
Spread batter in a greased 9x9x2-inch baking pan.
Bake at 400º F oven about 15 minutes or until top is golden.
Cool bread in pan for 10 minutes. Remove from pan by turning upside down on wire rack to cool completely.
Cut into 1/2 inch slices. Cut each slice into thirds.
Place in a single layer on a large, ungreased baking sheet and return to oven and bake for 8-10 minutes more or until crisp and all edges are golden brown. Cool. Makes approx. 40-50 cornbread pieces for dipping.

DIP

Quarter peppers; remove stems, seeds, and membranes. Place pieces on a baking sheet, lined with foil, skin side up.
Bake at 425º F for 20 minutes or until skins are blistered and dark.
Wrap in foil, set aside for 15 minutes. Peel off skin and discard.
Chop peppers finely.
While peppers are cooking and cooling, toss together cheese and flour in a medium bowl and set aside.
Cook onion in hot butter in a medium saucepan until onion is tender. Stir in half-and-half milk. Gradually add small amounts of the cheese mixture, stirring constantly over low heat until cheese is melted.
Stir in roasted peppers and jicama; heat through.
Transfer mixture to a small crock-pot or fondue pot over a fondue burner. Serve warm.

Approx. 8-10 servings

SAUSAGE and CHEESE BALLS

2 cups Bisquick (or any brand biscuit mix)
1 lb. ground sausage
1 cup grated Cheddar cheese

Mix all ingredients together in a medium bowl. Roll into bite-size balls.
Place on a cookie sheet and bake at 350º F for 15 to 20 minutes.

Makes approx. 30 balls

TOASTED PECANS

3 cups pecan halves
1 cup sugar
1 tsp cinnamon
1/2 tsp salt
1 1/2 tsp vanilla
5 tbsp water

Place pecans on a cookie sheet and bake at 350º F for 8 minutes.
In a medium saucepan, mix remaining ingredients and cook over medium
heat until mixture forms a soft ball.
Add pecans and stir until all are covered. Pour onto wax paper and
separate pecans. Allow to cool.
Transfer to a glass serving dish.

Makes about 3 cups of pecans

CAESAR TOAST

1 egg
1/4 cup Caesar Dressing
1 can Pillsbury Crescent Rolls (refrigerated)
2 cups herb-seasoned bread stuffing
1/3 cup grated Parmesan cheese

In a small bowl, combine egg and salad dressing; mix well.
Unroll crescent dough and separate into 8 triangles.
Cut each one in half lengthwise, forming 16 triangles.
Dip each triangle into salad dressing mixture, then put in crushed stuffing, and coat both sides.
Place 1 inch apart on an ungreased cookie sheet.
Sprinkle with Parmesan cheese.
Bake at 375º F for 12-15 minutes or until golden brown.

Makes 16 appetizers

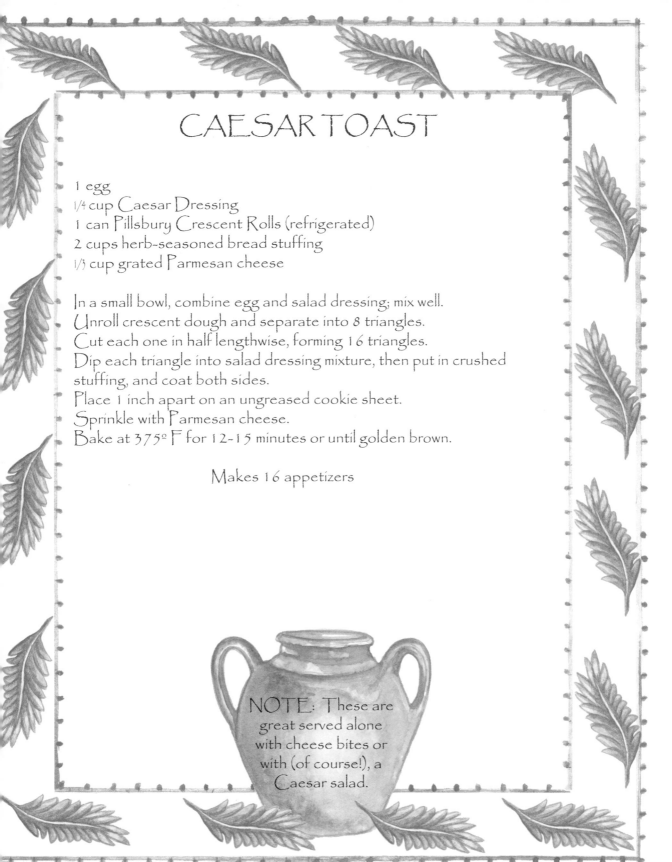

NOTE: These are great served alone with cheese bites or with (of course!), a Caesar salad.

FETA CHEESECAKE

1 cup ground walnuts
1/2 cup finely crushed zwieback toast
2 tbsp margarine or butter, melted
1 1/2 cups finely crumbled feta cheese
 flavored with basil and tomato (6 oz.)
1 5-oz. carton ricotta cheese
3 eggs
3/4 cup finely chopped fresh mushrooms
1/3 cup finely chopped pitted ripe olives
1/4 cup milk
1/2 tsp pepper
1/8 tsp salt
 Sliced ripe olives (optional)
 Fresh oregano leaves (optional)
 Fresh sliced vegetables (optional)

CRUST
Mix together walnuts, zwieback, and margarine or butter. Press onto the
bottom of a 9-inch springform pan.

FILLING
In a large bowl, beat feta and ricotta cheeses with an electric mixer on
medium speed until well combined. Add eggs all at once, beating on low
speed until just combined. Stir in mushrooms, chopped olives, milk,
pepper, and salt with a spoon. Pour filling into the springform pan, and
place on a larger shallow baking pan. Bake in a 325º F oven for 40 to
45 minutes or until the center appears nearly set when shaken. Cool for
15 minutes on a wire rack. Run a spatula around inside of the pan. Cool
for 30 minutes more. Remove side of pan. Cover and refrigerate at least
3 hours. Garnish cheesecake with sliced ripe olives and fresh oregano,
as desired. Serve with fresh sliced vegetables, if desired.

Makes 20 appetizer servings

NOTE: I like to use fat-free ricotta and feta cheese.

CRESCENT MUSHROOM BITES

1 tub soft cream cheese
1 pkg. crescent rolls, refrigerated
1 large jar sliced mushrooms, drained

Remove cream cheese from refrigerator and allow to warm slightly,
about 15 minutes. Unroll crescent rolls, separate into 2 squares.
Spread each square evenly with cream cheese.
Place an even layer of mushroom slices over cheese.
Roll up, jelly-roll fashion.
Slice and place on a cookie sheet.
Bake at 375° F for 15 minutes or until golden brown.

Makes about 24 appetizers

OK, so I can't
remember who, but it's

Somebody's *Favorite*

A cracker is just a cracker until you dip it or spread it with something delicious. The recipes in this section are some of our favorites. They are not meant just for snacking. As a special treat for the family one evening, why not try this: spread a large sheet of brown paper on the dinner table and crease it around the edges of the table so that it stays put. Lay out some crayons at each place setting. Then arrange an assortment of crackers on a serving platter. Include several different flavors and shapes. Serve up some of these great dips and spreads, some cornbread or French bread, and perhaps a big pot of soup, and voila! — Instant party! Even if it's just your family, it turns a casual dinner into a festive occasion. You can play "Pictionary" right on the table "cloth", or just let the kids have fun decorating it any way they like.

Some of our favorites are: Spinach Dip, Eggplant Dip, Hummus and Crab Spread. The truth is, though, there isn't one of these that we don't recommend!

Dips and Spreads

SPINACH  DIP

10-oz. pkg. chopped spinach, thawed, drained with water pressed out
1 pkg. dry vegetable soup mix, such a Knorr's
1 can water chestnuts, chopped and drained
1 cup mayonnaise
1 cup sour cream
1 large round loaf of pumpernickel bread, unsliced

Mix all ingredients together in a medium size bowl. Refrigerate overnight.
Slice off top crust of bread. Hollow out center and tear center piece into
bite-size pieces.
Spoon dip into hollowed out portion of bread and place on a large serving
dish. Surround with bread pieces.

Serves 8 to 10

DILL DIP

1 cup mayonnaise
2 tsp seasoned salt
1 cup sour cream
1 1/2 tbsp grated cheese
1 1/2 tsp dried parsley
1 1/2 tbsp dill weed

Blend all ingredients together.
Serve with cut raw vegetables.

Makes about 2 cups of dip

EGGPLANT DIP

1 medium eggplant (approx. 1 lb.)
2 tbsp olive oil
1 medium onion, chopped (1/2 cup)
1 14-oz. can stewed tomatoes
1/4 cup dry red wine vinegar
2 tbsp capers, drained
1/8 tsp salt
1/8 tsp black pepper
1 loaf of crusty or French bread (baguette)

Peel eggplant, if desired, and cut into 1/4-inch cubes. (You should have about 5 cups.)
In a large skillet, heat olive oil, add eggplant and onion. Cook, uncovered over medium-high heat about 10 minutes or until tender, stirring occasionally.
Stir in tomatoes, red wine vinegar, capers, salt and pepper.
Bring to a boil. Reduce heat. Simmer, uncovered, for 10 minutes or until liquid is evaporated.
Cool slightly; cover and chill for at least 3 hours.
Before serving, slice bread in small slices and arrange on a baking sheet.
Broil in oven turning once until toasted golden.

Makes about 4 cups of dip

CARROT DIP

1/2 of an 8-oz. carton sour cream
1/2 of an 8-oz. pkg. cream cheese, softened
1/4 cup mayonnaise
2 tsp soy sauce
1/4 tsp salt
1/4 tsp ground black pepper
1 1/2 cups finely shredded carrots
1/3 cup chopped green onions

In a mixing bowl, beat together sour cream, cream cheese, mayonnaise, soy sauce, salt and pepper with an electric mixer until smooth.
Stir in shredded carrots and green onions until combined.
Cover and chill for 4 to 24 hours. (Do not prepare any further ahead than this or it can become too thin).
Keep the dip chilled. Stir before serving. Serve with crackers, chips, celery sticks, or pita chips.

Makes about 2 cups of dip

CURRY DIP

1 clove garlic, minced
2 tbsp grated onion
1 pint mayonnaise
1 pinch salt
3 tbsp catsup
Dash of Tabasco sauce

Mix all ingredients together and chill for at least 1 hour.
Serve with raw vegetables such as celery, carrot sticks, cauliflower pieces, cut squash, and cherry tomatoes.

Makes 1 pint of dip

GUACAMOLE DIP

1 ripe avocado
2 tbsp lemon juice
1 tbsp chopped parsley
1/2 tsp salt

1 medium size ripe tomato
1 small garlic clove, mashed
2 green onions, finely chopped
Dash of pepper and salt to taste

In a small bowl, mash half the avocado with the lemon juice and chop the other half finely. Mix all the other ingredients together, including the chopped avocado, until well blended but still chunky. Cover and chill for at least 1 hour. Serve with tortilla chips.

Makes about 1 cup of dip

MEXICAN DIP

2 cans refried beans
1 1/2 lbs. ground beef
8-oz. bottle hot salsa
1 large onion, chopped
16-oz. carton sour cream
Green onions and black olives (chopped)

Spread refried beans in a large casserole dish.
Brown ground beef in skillet; drain well and spread over beans.
Pour salsa over ground beef.
Add chopped onions.
Cover all with sour cream.
Add chopped green onions and black olives on top, if desired.
Serve with tortilla chips.

Makes about 6 cups of dip

WALNUT SPREAD

1 cup canned garbanzo beans
1/2 cup chopped walnuts
1/2 cup lightly packed fresh basil leaves
2 tbsp olive oil
2 to 3 tsp lemon juice
Salt and pepper to taste
Pita bread slices or thin slices of crusty bread

Drain garbanzo beans, and reserve the liquid.
In a blender or food processor bowl, combine beans and 2 tbsp of the liquid, the walnuts, basil leaves, olive oil, lemon juice, salt and pepper.
Cover and blend or process until nearly smooth. You may add extra liquid if it is too stiff.
Serve on toasted slices of crusty bread or on pita slices.

Makes 1 to 1 1/4 cups spread

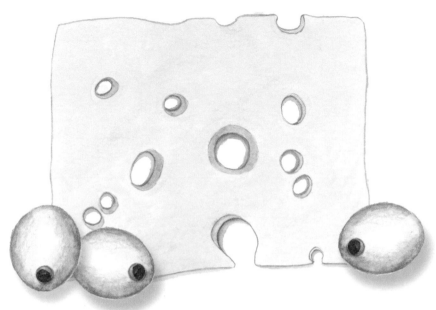

SWISS CHEESE and OLIVE SPREAD

3 cups Swiss cheese, shredded
3-oz. pkg. cream cheese, cut into cubes
1/4 cup dry white wine
3 tbsp mayonnaise
1 tsp Worcestershire sauce
1/3 cup chopped pitted ripe olives, drained
3 tbsp snipped Italian parsley
3 tbsp finely chopped green onion
Crackers

Place cheeses in a large bowl and let stand, covered, for 30 minutes at room temperature. Add wine, mayonnaise, and Worcestershire sauce.
Beat with an electric mixer until blended. Stir in olives, parsley and onion.
Place in a serving bowl, cover and chill for at least 2 hours. Let spread stand at room temperature for 1 hour before serving. Serve with crackers of your choice or cocktail bread slices.

Makes 10 to 12 servings

CRAB SPREAD

1 pint mayonnaise
2 tsp A-1 sauce
4 tbsp catsup
1/2 tsp curry powder
1 tbsp Parmesan cheese
1 lb. crabmeat

Mix all ingredients well and chill for several hours.
Serve with a variety of crackers.

Makes about 5 cups of spread

HUMMUS

15-oz. can chickpeas
  (garbanzo beans)
1/4 cup sesame paste (tahini)
1 tbsp lemon juice
2 to 4 cloves garlic

1/4 tsp salt
1/4 to 1/2 tsp ground red pepper
  (optional)
Pita bread, pita chips, bagel chips
  or carrot sticks

Drain liquid from chickpeas (reserving in case you want your hummus
thinner). Combine chickpeas, sesame paste, lemon juice, garlic, salt and
red pepper. Cover and process or blend until smooth. Liquid from
chickpeas may be added if you like a thinner consistency.
Spoon into a serving bowl. Serve with pita bread, chips or carrot sticks.

Makes 6 to 8 servings

EASY CHEESY DIP

1/2 block of Velveeta Cheese
1 can Ro-tel tomatoes and chilies

Cut Velveeta into 1/2-inch cubes.
Open Ro-tel tomatoes and drain.
Mix cubes and tomatoes and chilies in a medium bowl.
Microwave on high for 1-minute intervals, stirring in between
until dip is smooth and all cubes are melted.
Serve with tortilla chips or pita chips.

Makes about 2 1/2 cups of dip

FRUIT DIP

2 cups milk
3 1/4-oz. pkg. instant vanilla pudding mix
8-oz. container sour cream
Fresh fruit such as pineapple chunks,
 strawberries, banana chunks, green grapes

Yummy!

Combine milk and pudding mix, blend well; stir in sour cream.
Chill thoroughly and serve with fresh fruit.

Makes about 3 cups of dip

What could be more comforting on a cold or rainy night than a piping-hot bowl of soup or stew? I can't think of a thing. An added benefit for me is the fact that soups are so versatile that they can be easily modified. Add a bit more of this or that, a little more broth, or just double the recipe and you can feed a huge crowd at little expense. Some of our favorites are: Taco Soup, Chicken and Dumplings, Spinach and Mushroom Stew with Shrimp, and Red Pepper Fish Soup. My grown sons still get excited when they come over and there is hot soup simmering on the stove. It feels like home.

Soups

VEGETABLE SOUP

3 cans vegetable broth, or chicken broth
2 cups potatoes, peeled, and cut into cubes
1 medium onion, chopped
1 large pkg. frozen mixed vegetables
2 cans diced tomatoes
Pinch of sugar
Salt and pepper to taste

Pour vegetable broth into a large soup pot.
Add potatoes and onion.
Cook over medium-high heat until potatoes are tender.
Add frozen vegetables and tomatoes; bring to boiling.
Add pinch of sugar.
Reduce heat and simmer 20 minutes.
Salt and pepper to taste.

Serves 10

SAVE
the World
the Whales
the Leftovers

RED PEPPER and FISH SOUP

1 1/4 lbs. cod or red snapper, frozen or fresh
1 medium sweet red pepper, chopped
1 medium sweet yellow pepper, chopped
1 medium sweet orange pepper, chopped
1 cup chopped onion
2 tbsp olive oil
3 14-oz. cans chicken broth
1/4 tsp salt
1/2 tsp black pepper
1/2 cup snipped fresh Italian parsley

Thaw fish if frozen, rinse and pat dry. Cut each piece into 1-inch pieces and set aside.

In a large saucepan, cook sweet peppers and onion in hot oil over medium heat for 5 minutes. Add one can of the chicken broth. Bring to boil; reduce heat. Simmer, covered about 20 minutes or until peppers are very tender. Remove from heat, cool.

Place half the pepper mixture in a food processor. Cover and blend until nearly smooth. Repeat with remaining pepper mixture. Return all to the saucepan.

Add remaining broth, salt, and pepper. Add fish to broth.

Bring to boiling; reduce heat. Simmer covered about 5 minutes or until fish flakes when tested with a fork. Stir in snipped parsley.

Makes about 9 cups of soup

VEGETABLE DUMPLINGS

3 cans fat-free chicken broth
2 cups water
2 tbsp salt
1 pkg. pre-cut, pre-washed potato chunks
9-oz. pkg. frozen Pictsweet brand peas in butter
9-oz. pkg. frozen Pictsweet brand carrots in butter
9-oz. pkg. frozen Pictsweet brand corn in butter
1 cup fat-free half-and-half
Dash pepper

DUMPLINGS
2 cups flour
1/2 cup plus milk

Place broth, water, salt in a large soup pot and bring to a
rolling boil. Add potatoes. Boil for 10 minutes. Add all
other vegetables. Lower heat to medium and simmer for 15 minutes.
Mix dumpling ingredients in a medium bowl until stiff dough forms.
On a floured surface, roll out the dough to about 1/2-inch
thick. Cut into strips. Return broth to boil. Holding strip
of dough in your hand, pinch into 1-inch pieces and drop
into boiling broth until all strips are dropped into broth.
Lower heat to medium-high and cook for 10 minutes.
Add half-and-half and sprinkle with pepper.

Serves 8 to 10

CHICKEN and POTATO SOUP

Chicken, 1 whole or 3 breasts
5 potatoes
1 medium onion, chopped
Salt and pepper to taste
1 cup half-and-half or 13-oz. can evaporated milk

In a large soup pot, boil chicken until tender.
Remove from broth and allow to cool. Save broth.
Remove chicken from bones and chop into chunks.
In the meantime, cook potatoes and onion in broth on high about 20
minutes. Add chicken and milk to pot, allow to return to boil,
and then reduce heat to simmer for 10 minutes. Stir and
serve.

Serves 8 to 10

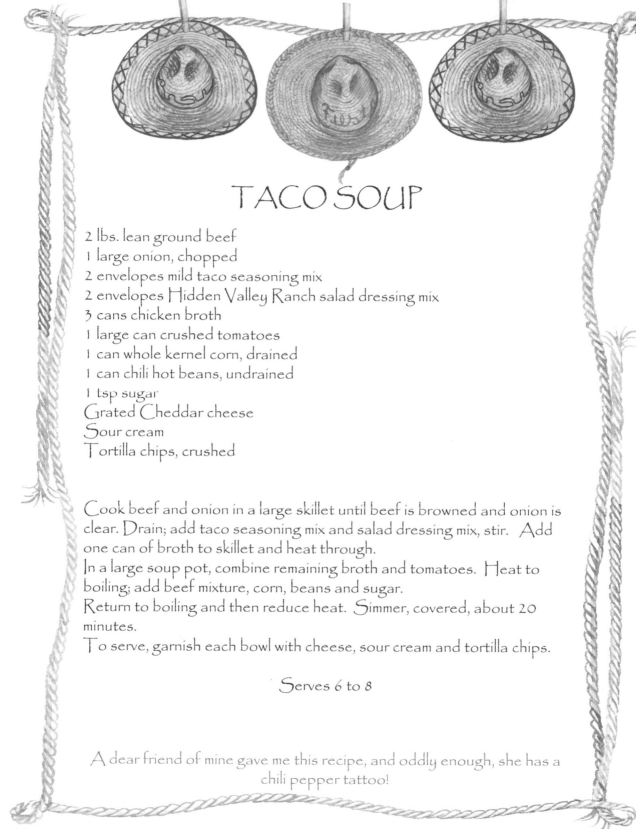

TACO SOUP

2 lbs. lean ground beef
1 large onion, chopped
2 envelopes mild taco seasoning mix
2 envelopes Hidden Valley Ranch salad dressing mix
3 cans chicken broth
1 large can crushed tomatoes
1 can whole kernel corn, drained
1 can chili hot beans, undrained
1 tsp sugar
Grated Cheddar cheese
Sour cream
Tortilla chips, crushed

Cook beef and onion in a large skillet until beef is browned and onion is clear. Drain; add taco seasoning mix and salad dressing mix, stir. Add one can of broth to skillet and heat through.
In a large soup pot, combine remaining broth and tomatoes. Heat to boiling; add beef mixture, corn, beans and sugar.
Return to boiling and then reduce heat. Simmer, covered, about 20 minutes.
To serve, garnish each bowl with cheese, sour cream and tortilla chips.

Serves 6 to 8

A dear friend of mine gave me this recipe, and oddly enough, she has a chili pepper tattoo!

CAULIFLOWER CHOWDER

1 large onion, chopped
2 tbsp butter or margarine
2 cups peeled, diced potatoes
4 cups vegetable broth or chicken broth
2 1/2 cups cauliflower florets
1 cup half-and-half
2 tbsp all-purpose flour
Salt and pepper to taste
3 cups shredded Swiss cheese
2 tbsp snipped fresh Italian parsley

In a large soup pot, cook onion in butter until clear.
Add potatoes and cook for 3 to 5 minutes, add broth. Bring to boiling.
Reduce heat, cover and simmer for 6 minutes.
Add cauliflower and return to boiling.
Reduce heat, cover and simmer for 6 minutes more, or until vegetables are tender.
In a small bowl, whisk half-and-half into flour until smooth.
Add to soup mixture.
Cook and stir until mixture is thickened. Reduce heat to low.
Stir in 2 1/2 cups of cheese until melted. Do not boil.
Season with salt and pepper to taste.
At serving, garnish each bowl with remaining cheese and parsley.

Serves 6 to 8

EASY CHICKEN and DUMPLINGS

1 rotisserie chicken (traditional or herb)
3 cans fat-free chicken broth
2 cups water
2 tbsp salt
1 cup fat-free half-and-half
Dash pepper

DUMPLINGS
2 cups flour
1/2 cup plus milk

Remove all meat from chicken; discard skin and bones.
Place broth, water, salt and chicken meat in a large soup pot and bring to a rolling boil.
Lower heat to medium and simmer for 10 minutes.
Mix dumpling ingredients in a medium bowl until stiff dough forms.
On a floured surface, roll out the dough to about 1/2-inch thick. Cut into strips.
Return broth to boil.
Holding strip of dough in your hand, pinch into 1-inch pieces and drop into boiling broth until all strips are dropped into broth.
Lower heat to medium-high and cook for 10 minutes.
Add half-and-half and sprinkle with pepper.

Serves 8 to 10

SPINACH and MUSHROOM STEW with SHRIMP

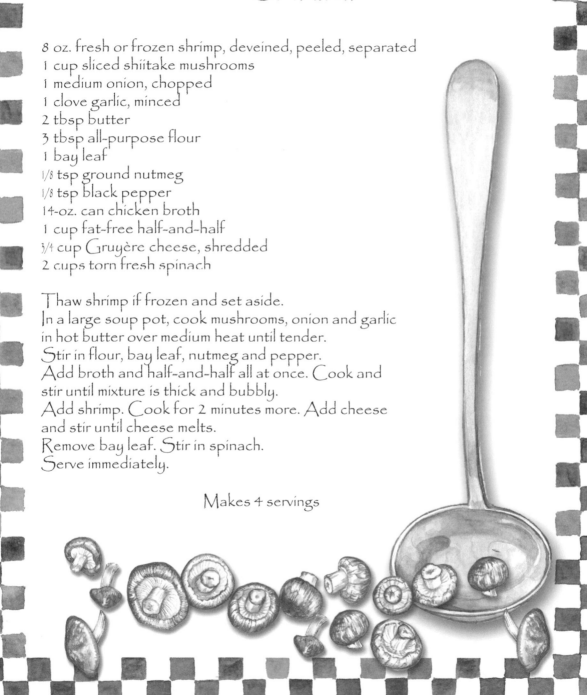

8 oz. fresh or frozen shrimp, deveined, peeled, separated
1 cup sliced shiitake mushrooms
1 medium onion, chopped
1 clove garlic, minced
2 tbsp butter
3 tbsp all-purpose flour
1 bay leaf
1/8 tsp ground nutmeg
1/8 tsp black pepper
14-oz. can chicken broth
1 cup fat-free half-and-half
3/4 cup Gruyère cheese, shredded
2 cups torn fresh spinach

Thaw shrimp if frozen and set aside.
In a large soup pot, cook mushrooms, onion and garlic
in hot butter over medium heat until tender.
Stir in flour, bay leaf, nutmeg and pepper.
Add broth and half-and-half all at once. Cook and
stir until mixture is thick and bubbly.
Add shrimp. Cook for 2 minutes more. Add cheese
and stir until cheese melts.
Remove bay leaf. Stir in spinach.
Serve immediately.

Makes 4 servings

CREAMY POTATO SOUP

4 to 5 large potatoes
2 quarts water
1 tsp salt
1/4 cup butter or margarine
2 tbsp flour
1/4 cup water
1 cup half-and-half
Salt and pepper to taste
1 cup shredded Cheddar cheese, if desired

Peel and chop potatoes.
Place in a large soup pot with water and 1 tsp salt.
Bring to boil, lower heat to medium-low and cook until potatoes are soft.
Add butter.
In a small bowl, mix flour with 1/4 cup water until smooth, add to potatoes,
and stir until slightly thickened. Add half-and-half; heat through.
Salt and pepper to taste.
If desired, sprinkle cheese on top of each serving.

Serves 6

HOMEMADE CHICKEN NOODLE SOUP

2 14-oz. cans chicken broth
2 cups water
3 carrots, chopped
2 ribs celery, chopped
Dash of pepper
3 slices fresh ginger root
1 tbsp vegetable oil
1/2 cup chopped cooked chicken
1/2 cup egg noodles

In a large soup pot over medium heat, combine broth, water, carrots, celery and pepper.
Simmer until carrots are tender.
In the meantime, in a medium skillet over medium-high heat, combine the ginger, oil and chicken. Sauté for 5 minutes and remove the sliced ginger.
Add the chicken to the broth mixture and bring to boiling. Add noodles.
Cook over medium heat for about 15 minutes or until noodles are tender.

Makes 4 servings

FRENCH ONION SOUP

1/2 cup butter
2 tbsp olive oil
4 cups sliced onions
4 10 1/2-oz. cans beef broth
1 tsp dried thyme

Salt and pepper to taste
1 large loaf French bread, sliced
6 slices Provolone cheese
3/4 cup shredded Swiss cheese
1/4 cup grated Parmesan cheese

Melt butter in a large soup pot on medium heat.
Add olive oil and stir in onions. Cook until onions
are clear, but do not brown. Add beef broth and
thyme. Season with salt and pepper.
Simmer 30 minutes. Toast bread in the oven.
Pour soup into individual oven-safe bowls. Place
one slice of the toasted French bread on top of
each bowl. Add 1 slice of Provolone, the
shredded Swiss and Parmesan and broil in the
oven until the cheese is bubbly.

Makes 4 to 6 servings

POST CARD

PARIS IS HERE
WISH YOU
WERE,
BEAUTIFUL

TOMATO BASIL SOUP

3 cans whole peeled tomatoes
2 tbsp olive oil
2 zucchini, cubed
2 large onions, chopped
2 cups fresh sliced mushrooms
2 tbsp salt
3 bay leaves
1/2 tsp dried thyme
2 tsp dried basil
1/2 tsp ground white pepper
2 to 3 tbsp fresh basil, chopped

In a food processor, purée whole tomatoes until smooth.
In a large soup pot, cook zucchini, onions and mushrooms in olive oil over medium heat until tender. Pour in the puréed tomatoes.
Season with salt, bay leaves, thyme, basil and pepper.
Bring to boiling, then reduce heat and simmer 14 minutes.
Remove bay leaves. Just before serving, add fresh basil and stir.

Makes 10 servings

Ahhh, salads! They offer up everything that is good for you. Eating without guilt. I love salads of any kind. They are a feast for the eyes and the taste buds. And besides, how many foods can you "toss" and still be able to place on a dish and serve? On a warm summer day especially, choose three of these and serve them with some of the sandwiches mentioned later on, and you have a light and easy lunch or dinner for a crowd. And whether stirred, tossed, layered or mixed, these are all wonderful. Hope you think so too.

Salads

SEVEN LAYER SALAD

1 large head iceberg lettuce
1 cup chopped celery
1 cup chopped green pepper
1 large onion, chopped
1 pkg. frozen peas, thawed
1 cup mayonnaise
1/2 cup grated Parmesan cheese
1/2 cup bacon bits

Chop lettuce and place half in the bottom of a deep, clear glass salad bowl.
Top with a layer of celery, green pepper, onion and peas, in that order.
Cover with the remaining lettuce. Spread mayonnaise over lettuce.
Sprinkle with cheese, then bacon bits. Cover and refrigerate for 24 hours before serving.

Makes 8 servings

AVOCADO SALAD

1 medium head iceberg lettuce, torn
2 cups torn red leaf lettuce
1 medium ripe avocado, peeled and sliced
1/4 cup orange juice
1 cucumber, sliced
1/2 medium red onion, thinly sliced
1 can (11-oz.) mandarin oranges, drained

DRESSING
1/2 cup orange juice
1/4 cup vegetable oil
2 tbsp red wine vinegar
1 tbsp sugar
1 tsp grated orange peel
1/4 tsp salt

In a jar with tight-fitting lid, combine dressing ingredients; shake well. Chill. Just before serving, toss greens in a large salad bowl. Dip the avocado slices into orange juice; arrange over greens (discard remaining juice). Add cucumber, onion and oranges. Serve with dressing.

Serves 6

SUMMER SQUASH SALAD

4 cups julienne zucchini squash
4 cups julienne yellow squash
2 cups radishes, sliced
2 cups vegetable oil
1/3 cup cider vinegar
2 tbsp Dijon mustard
2 tbsp snipped fresh parsley
1 1/2 tsp salt
1 tsp dill weed
1/2 tsp pepper

In a large bowl, toss zucchini, yellow squash and radishes.
In a jar with a tight fitting lid, combine all remaining ingredients; shake well.
Pour over squash. Cover and refrigerate for at least 2 hours.

Makes 12 servings

MACARONI SALAD

2 stalks celery ribs, chopped
1/2 small onion, chopped
1/2 cup mayonnaise
1 tbsp white vinegar
1 tbsp sugar
1 tsp salt
1 tsp prepared mustard
1/2 tsp pepper
4 cups cooked elbow macaroni
2 hard-boiled eggs, chopped
1/2 cup chopped sweet red pepper

Mix together first eight ingredients in a large mixing bowl.
Add macaroni, eggs and red pepper. Mix lightly. Chill for at least
1 hour.
Transfer into a serving bowl and serve.

Makes 6 servings

SOUTHERN BEAN SALAD

1 5-1/2 oz. can kidney beans, drained and rinsed
1 5-1/2 oz. can black beans, drained and rinsed
1 5-1/2 oz. can garbanzo beans, drained and
  rinsed
2 celery ribs, sliced
1 medium red onion, diced
1 medium ripe tomato, diced
1 cup frozen whole kernel corn, thawed

DRESSING
3/4 cup salsa, think and chunky
1/4 cup vegetable oil
1/2 cup lime juice
1 1/2 tsp chili powder
1 tsp salt
1/2 tsp ground cumin

In a large bowl, combine beans, celery, onion, tomato and corn.
In a small bowl, combine dressing ingredients; mix well.
Pour dressing over bean mixture and toss to coat. Cover.
Chill for at least 2 hours before serving.

Serves 10

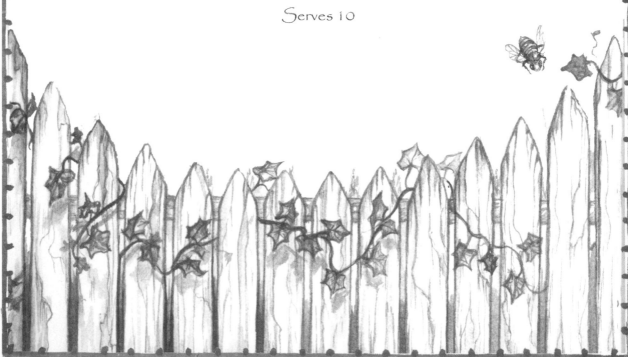

WILD RICE SALAD

DRESSING
1/4 cup olive oil or vegetable oil
1/3 cup orange juice
2 tbsp honey

SALAD
1 cup wild rice, uncooked
2 golden delicious apples, chopped
Juice of 1 lemon
1 cup golden raisins
1 cup seedless red grapes, halved
2 tbsp fresh mint
2 tbsp parsley
2 tbsp chives
Dash of salt and pepper
1 cup pecans

Combine dressing ingredients and set aside.
Cook rice according to package directions; drain if needed and allow to cool.
In a large bowl, toss apples with lemon juice. Add raisins, grapes, mint, parsley, chives and cooked rice. Add dressing and toss. Season with salt and pepper.
Cover and chill for several hours or overnight.
Just before serving add pecans and toss lightly.

Makes 8 - 10 servings

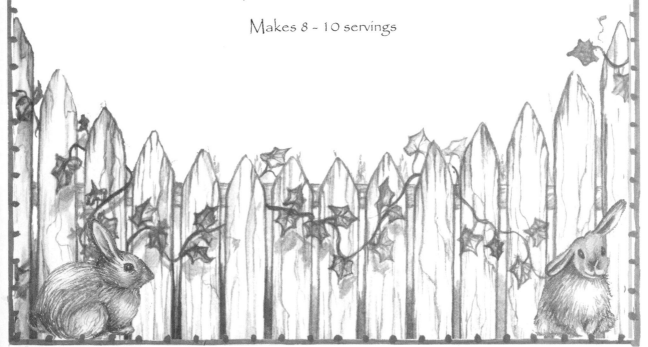

THREE BEAN SALAD

1 6-oz. can French-style green beans, drained
 and rinsed
1 6-oz. can wax beans, drained and rinsed
1 6-oz. can kidney beans, drained and rinsed
1/2 cup chopped onion
8-oz. bottle Italian salad dressing
1 tbsp sugar
2 garlic cloves, minced
Crisp lettuce leaves

In a large bowl, with tight-fitting lid, combine all beans and onion.
In a small bowl, combine salad dressing, sugar and garlic. Pour over bean
mixture and toss.
Cover and refrigerate at least 3 hours, stirring occasionally.
Just before serving, remove bean mixture with a slotted spoon to a
lettuce-lined salad bowl.

Serves 6

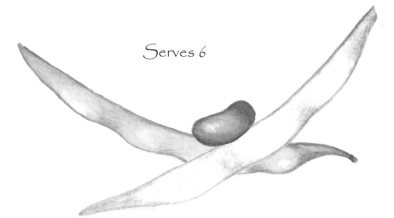

ENGLISH PEA SALAD

2 cans English peas, drained
2 hard-boiled eggs, sliced
1 cup cubed Colby cheese
1/2 medium onion, finely chopped
1/4 tsp celery salt
Dash of pepper
Mayonnaise

Combine all ingredients in a large mixing bowl.
Add mayonnaise, using enough to coat well. Transfer
to serving bowl. Chill for 1 to 2 hours.

Serves 4

SEVEN-CUP SALAD 7

1 cup chopped nuts
1 cup cottage cheese
1 cup flaked coconut
1 cup pineapple chunks
1 cup fruit cocktail
1 cup sour cream
1 cup colored miniature
marshmallows

Mix together all ingredients in a large bowl with lid.
Chill overnight.
Just before serving, transfer to a serving dish.

Makes 6 servings

COPPER PENNIES

6 red bell peppers, sliced
1 large onion, sliced
2 lbs. sliced carrots, cooked, drained and cooled
3/4 cup vinegar
1 tsp prepared mustard
1/2 cup vegetable oil
1 cup sugar
1 can tomato soup, undiluted

Place peppers, onion and carrots in a large bowl.
Mix vinegar, mustard, oil, sugar and tomato soup in a
medium saucepan. Bring to a boil.
Pour over carrots, peppers and onions.
Chill in refrigerator for 24 hours.

Makes 6 servings

No, of course we aren't eating REAL copper pennies!! Then we would have no 'cents' at all!!!

PASTA SALAD
with GARLIC MAYO

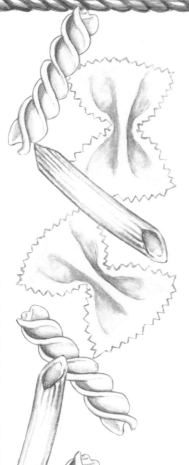

9 oz. penne pasta
1 tbsp olive oil
8 medium Fuji apples
Juice of 4 lemons
1 bunch of celery stalks, sliced
3/4 cup walnut halves
1 bag pre-washed and pre-cut spring mix
  salad

GARLIC MAYONNAISE
2 egg yolks
Pinch of salt
6 garlic cloves, crushed
1 1/2 cups vegetable oil
1 to 2 tbsp white wine vinegar
1 tsp Dijon mustard
Salt to taste

Cook pasta in a large saucepan with salt and olive oil until tender, about 8-10 minutes. Drain, then run cool water over, drain again and then set aside. Core and dice apples, place in a medium bowl and sprinkle with lemon juice.

To make the garlic mayonnaise, beat together the 2 egg yolks, pinch of salt and garlic. Beat in oil, 2 to 3 tbsp at a time. When 1/4 has been incorporated, beat in 1 to 2 tbsp vinegar. Continue beating in the oil. Stir in Dijon mustard and salt to taste.

Mix together the pasta, apples, celery and walnuts.

Toss with the garlic mayonnaise until coated.

Line a salad serving bowl with salad mixture and spoon the pasta salad into the lined bowl before serving.

Makes 4 servings

AVOCADO, TOMATO and FRESH MOZZARELLA SALAD

6 oz. bowtie pasta
6 ripe fresh tomatoes
8 oz. fresh mozzarella cheese
1 large ripe avocado
2 tbsp pine nuts, toasted

DRESSING
6 tbsp olive oil
2 tbsp red wine vinegar
1 tsp whole grain mustard
Pinch of sugar
Salt and pepper to taste
2 tbsp chopped basil

Cook pasta according to package directions in salted water. Drain and cool. Slice the tomatoes and mozzarella into thin round slices.
Halve the avocado, remove the stone and peel off the skin. Cut into lengthwise slices.
In a small bowl, whisk together all the dressing ingredients, except for the basil.
On a large round plate, arrange alternate slices of mozzarella, avocado and tomato in a spiral pattern, overlapping slightly.
Toss the pasta with half the dressing and the chopped basil.
Place in the center of the plate.
Pour remaining dressing over the tomatoes, cheese and avocado slices and garnish with the pine nuts, and a sprig of fresh basil, if you wish.

Makes 4 servings

HAWAIIAN RICE SALAD

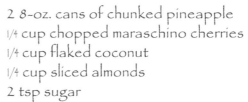

2 8-oz. cans of chunked pineapple
1/4 cup chopped maraschino cherries
1/4 cup flaked coconut
1/4 cup sliced almonds
2 tsp sugar
1/4 cup sour cream
1 tsp salt
3 cups rice, cooked

Drain pineapple, reserving 1/4 cup of
juice. Cut chunks in half.
Combine pineapple, cherries, coconut,
and almonds in a medium bowl.
Blend in sugar, sour cream, salt and
reserved pineapple juice.
Pour over rice and toss till mixed.

Makes 6 servings

BLUEBERRY SALAD

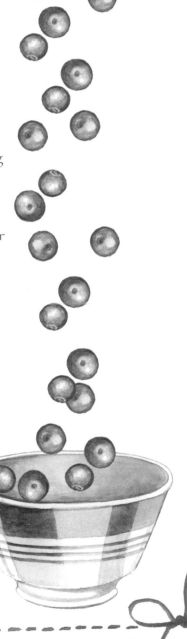

1 small can blueberries (drain and save juice)
1 small can crushed pineapple (drain and save juice)
1 large pkg. cherry Jell-O
1/2 pint sour cream
1 8-oz. pkg. cream cheese
1/2 cup mayonnaise
1 tsp vanilla
1/2 cup sugar
1 cup chopped nuts

To reserved juices, add enough water to make
3 1/2 cups of liquid. Pour into a medium saucepan; bring
to a boil and dissolve Jell-O into juices.
Allow to cool.
Add pineapple and blueberries. Chill until firm.
In a blender (or with mixer in a medium bowl), blend sour
cream and cream cheese.
Add mayonnaise, vanilla, sugar and nuts.
Turn into large, clear glass dish such as a trifle bowl.
Cover sour cream and cheese mixture with the Jell-O
mixture and chill overnight.

Serves 6

WATERMELON SALAD

Don't forget to take out the seeds!

1/4 lb. prosciutto, cut into very thin pieces
2 tbsp chopped fresh basil
4 tbsp balsamic vinegar
3 tsp honey
1/8 tsp paprika
1/3 cup olive oil
3 cups watermelon, peeled, seeded and cubed
2 large bunches watercress
1/2 tsp black pepper

Line the bottom of a large platter with the prosciutto.
In a small bowl, mix basil, vinegar, honey, paprika and olive oil with a wire whisk.
In a large bowl, place watermelon and watercress. Pour dressing over and toss lightly.
Place salad on top of prosciutto on platter; sprinkle with pepper.

Makes 4 servings

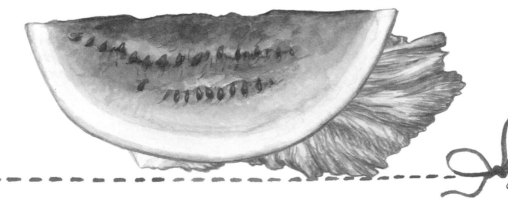

"Eat your vegetables!" Well, these recipes are bound to make it easier. Vegetables are so colorful that the artist in me loves to look at them, as well find creative ways to cook them. And let's face it, with children (and some adults, for that matter), making them a bit more interesting is key. My stepsons were not vegetable eaters when I first met them, unless it was potatoes. During those early years, with all of us together, when it came time to prepare mashed potatoes for dinner, whoever was on my "bad" list got the task of peeling and cutting up the potatoes. That meant a 5 lb-bag! Over time though, I won them over with the squash, broccoli and green bean casseroles presented here. And they will all admit (me included), that no one can cook baked beans like their sister Bethany.

Vegetables
and
Side Dishes

SQUASH-CARROT CASSEROLE

2 lbs. yellow summer squash
1/4 cup chopped onion
1 can cream of chicken soup
1 cup sour cream
1 cup shredded carrots
8-oz. package herb-seasoned stuffing mix
1/2 cup butter or margarine, melted

In a medium saucepan, cook squash and onion in boiling water, about 5 minutes; drain.
In a large bowl, combine soup and sour cream. Stir in shredded carrots.
Fold in drained squash and onion.
In a small bowl, combine stuffing mix and melted butter or margarine.
Spread half of stuffing in bottom of a 13x9x2-inch baking dish.
Spoon vegetable mixture evenly over stuffing, and sprinkle remaining stuffing on top.
Bake at 350º F for 25 to 30 minutes.

Serves 6

SWEET POTATO SOUFFLÉ

2 large cans yams
1 cup sugar
1/4 tsp salt
1/2 tsp vanilla
2 eggs
1/2 stick margarine
1/2 cup milk

In a large bowl, mix all ingredients together
with an electric mixer.
Pour into a 13x9x2-inch baking dish.

TOPPING
1 cup brown sugar
1 cup chopped nuts
1/3 cup flour
1/3 stick margarine

Mix topping ingredients together in a medium
size bowl until well blended.
Pour evenly over sweet potato mixture.
Bake at 350º F for 35 minutes.

Serves 8 to 10

AKA. SWEET POTATO SHUFFLE

BETHANY'S BAKED BEANS

3 14-oz. cans baked beans
1/3 cup catsup
3 tbsp yellow or Dijon mustard
1/2 cup light brown sugar
Salt and pepper to taste

Mix all ingredients together in a large bowl.
Pour into a greased 2-quart baking dish.
Bake at 350º F for 40 minutes. Serve warm.

Makes 8 to 10 servings

BROCCOLI and RICE CASSEROLE

10-oz. pkg. frozen broccoli, cooked and drained
1 cup cooked rice
1 can cream of chicken soup
1 can sliced water chestnuts
8-oz. jar of Cheez Whiz
1 cup crushed cracker crumbs

Mix first five ingredients together in a bowl.
Place in a baking dish and top with cracker
crumbs.
Bake for 30 minutes at 350º F.

Serves 8

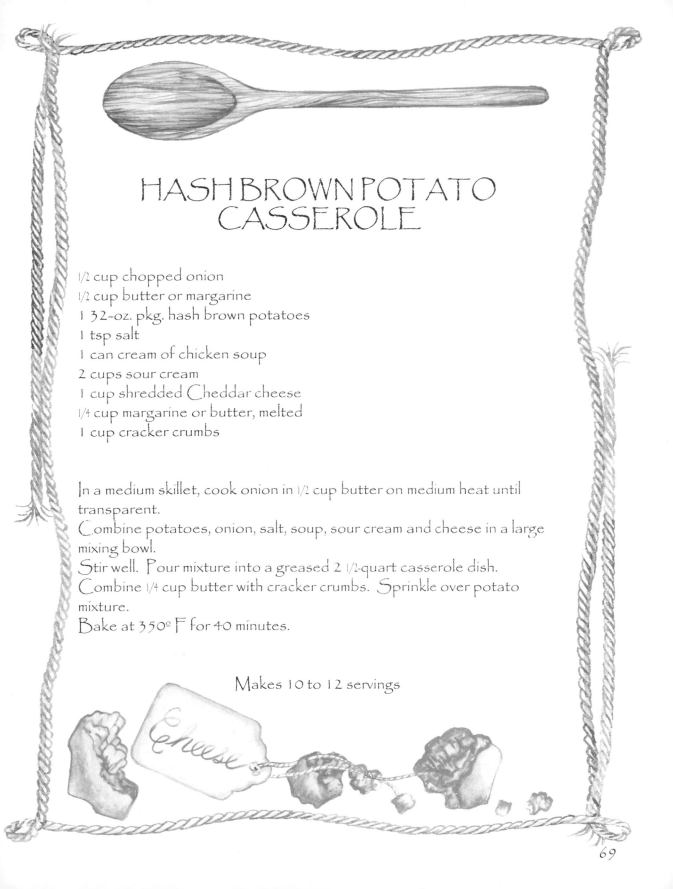

HASH BROWN POTATO CASSEROLE

1/2 cup chopped onion
1/2 cup butter or margarine
1 32-oz. pkg. hash brown potatoes
1 tsp salt
1 can cream of chicken soup
2 cups sour cream
1 cup shredded Cheddar cheese
1/4 cup margarine or butter, melted
1 cup cracker crumbs

In a medium skillet, cook onion in 1/2 cup butter on medium heat until transparent.
Combine potatoes, onion, salt, soup, sour cream and cheese in a large mixing bowl.
Stir well. Pour mixture into a greased 2 1/2-quart casserole dish.
Combine 1/4 cup butter with cracker crumbs. Sprinkle over potato mixture.
Bake at 350º F for 40 minutes.

Makes 10 to 12 servings

BUTTERNUT SQUASH CASSEROLE

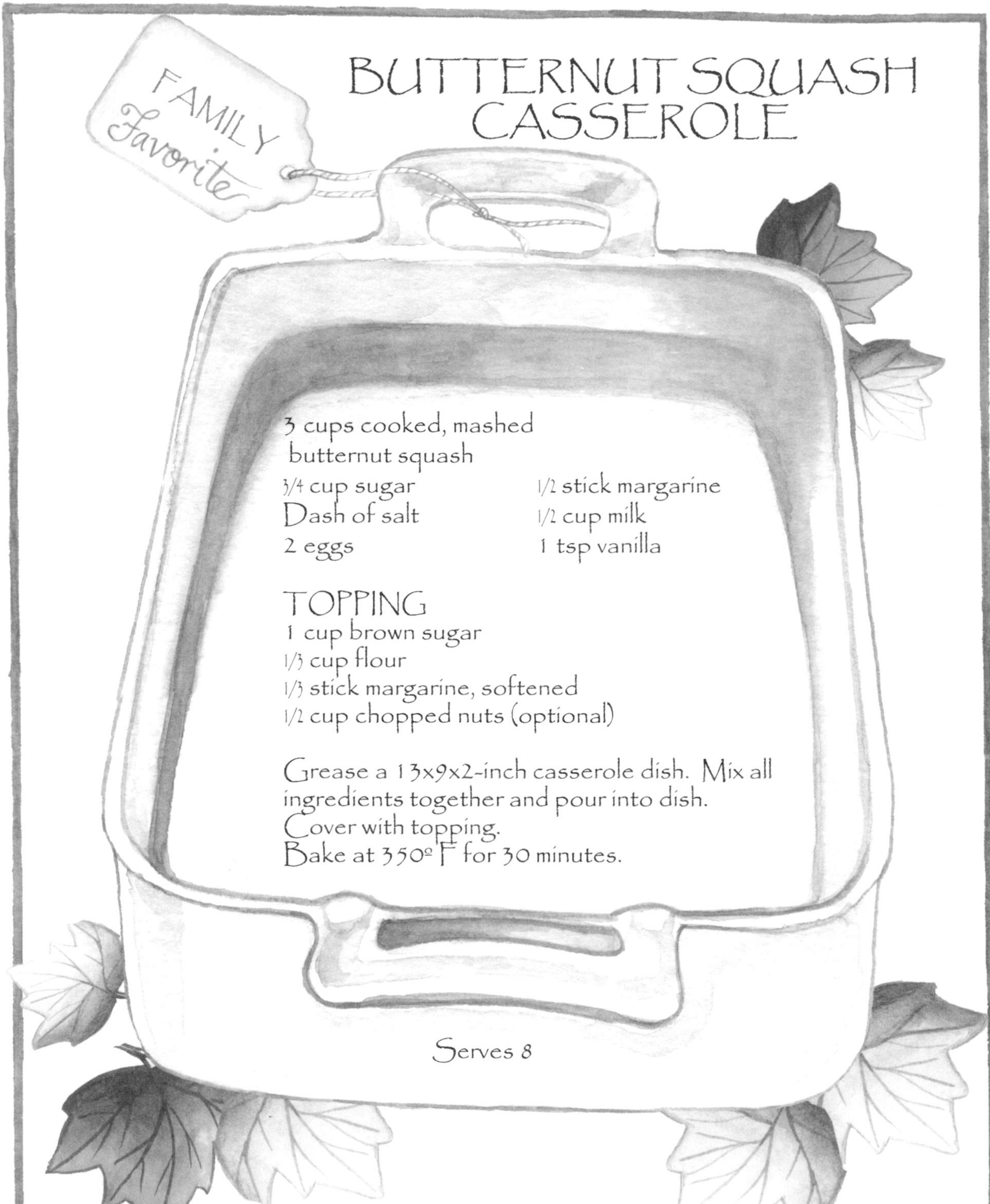

FAMILY Favorite

3 cups cooked, mashed
 butternut squash

3/4 cup sugar	1/2 stick margarine
Dash of salt	1/2 cup milk
2 eggs	1 tsp vanilla

TOPPING
1 cup brown sugar
1/3 cup flour
1/3 stick margarine, softened
1/2 cup chopped nuts (optional)

Grease a 13x9x2-inch casserole dish. Mix all
ingredients together and pour into dish.
Cover with topping.
Bake at 350º F for 30 minutes.

Serves 8

CANDIED  CARROTS

1 lb. carrots
1 chicken bouillon cube
1/2 cup boiling water
1 tbsp margarine
1/4 cup light corn syrup

Peel carrots and cut into small pieces.
In a medium saucepan, dissolve bouillon cube in boiling water; add margarine,
syrup and carrots.
Cover and cook over medium heat for 10 minutes.
Uncover and cook for 10 minutes more or until carrots are tender and glazed
liquid is absorbed.

Serves 6 ~ 8

COLESLAW

1 medium cabbage, chopped fine
1/2 tsp salt
1/2 cup vinegar
1/2 cup vegetable oil

1 tbsp prepared mustard
1/2 cup sugar
1 tsp celery seed

Place chopped cabbage in a bowl with a
tight fitting cover.
Combine salt, vinegar, oil, mustard, sugar
and celery seed in a small saucepan; bring to
boil, stirring to dissolve sugar.
Pour over cabbage; toss lightly. Cover and
chill overnight.

Serves 6

MASHED POTATOES

Don't put the peelings in the disposal!

6 large Idaho baking potatoes
3 chicken bouillon cubes
Butter or margarine
Salt and pepper to taste
8-oz. pkg. cream cheese
1/2 cup sour cream
1 cup plus half-and-half

Peel potatoes and cut into chunks. In a large saucepan, place potatoes, bouillon cubes and water to cover.
Cook on high until potatoes are tender.
Drain and place in a large mixing bowl.
Add butter, salt and pepper to your own taste.
Add cream cheese, sour cream and half-and-half.
Using an electric mixer, whip until blended and fluffy. If you wish, you may put more butter in the center at serving.

Serves 6 to 8

CREOLE CABBAGE

1 lb. lean ground beef
1 medium onion, chopped
1 can whole tomatoes
1 can Cheddar cheese soup
Salt and pepper to taste
1/2 tsp chili powder
1/2 cup water
1 can Ro-tel tomatoes with chilies
1 head cabbage, chopped

In a large skillet, cook ground beef with onion until beef is browned and onion is clear.
Drain.
Add all other ingredients, except cabbage. Simmer over medium-low heat for 10 minutes.
Add cabbage and simmer until cabbage is done.
Serve over crumbled cornbread, or over rice.

Serves 6

CORN CASSEROLE

1 can whole kernel corn, undrained
1 can creamed corn
1 stick butter, melted
2 eggs, beaten
1 tbsp sugar
1 cup sour cream
1 tbsp chopped onion
1 box Jiffy brand cornbread muffin mix
Dash salt and pepper

Mix all ingredients together in a large bowl.
Stir until well blended.
Pour mixture into a greased 13x9x2-inch casserole dish.
Bake at 350º F for 45 minutes.

Serves 6

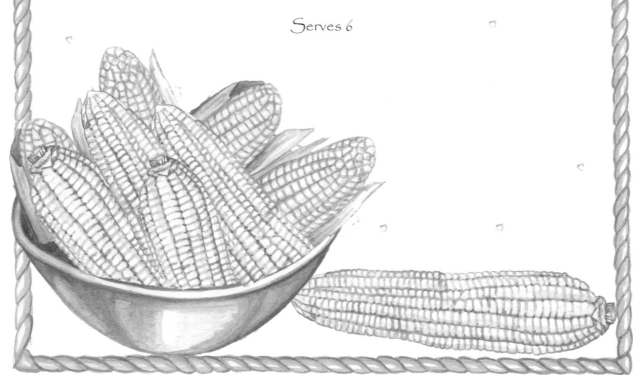

GREEN BEAN CASSEROLE

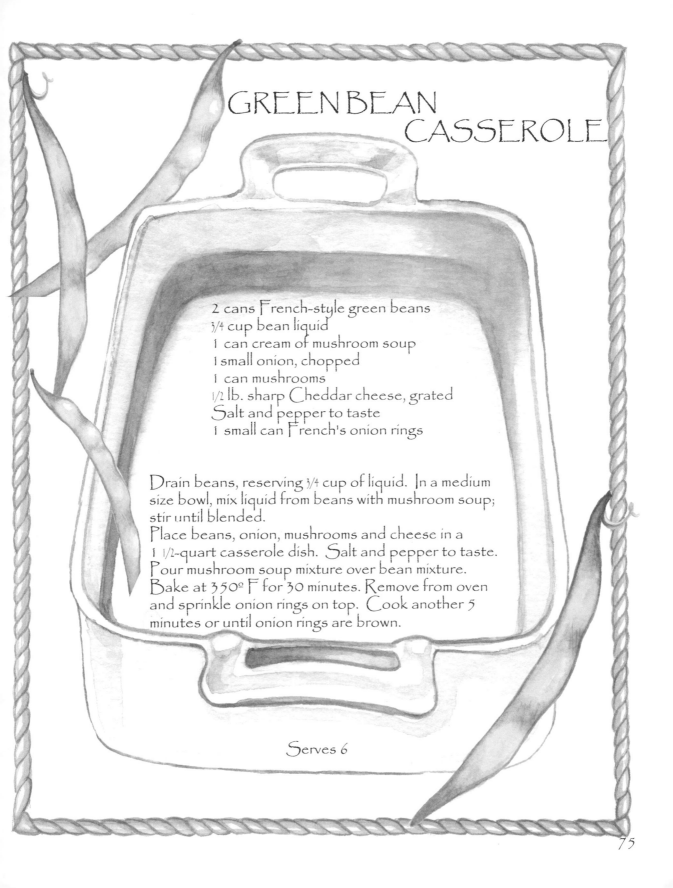

2 cans French-style green beans
3/4 cup bean liquid
1 can cream of mushroom soup
1 small onion, chopped
1 can mushrooms
1/2 lb. sharp Cheddar cheese, grated
Salt and pepper to taste
1 small can French's onion rings

Drain beans, reserving 3/4 cup of liquid. In a medium size bowl, mix liquid from beans with mushroom soup; stir until blended.
Place beans, onion, mushrooms and cheese in a 1 1/2-quart casserole dish. Salt and pepper to taste. Pour mushroom soup mixture over bean mixture. Bake at 350º F for 30 minutes. Remove from oven and sprinkle onion rings on top. Cook another 5 minutes or until onion rings are brown.

Serves 6

BROCCOLI CASSEROLE

1 large stalk broccoli, cooked
1 can cream of mushroom soup
1 cup mayonnaise
2 eggs, beaten
2 tbsp chopped onion
1 cup grated sharp Cheddar cheese
1 cup crushed cheese crackers

Chop cooked broccoli into chunks;
place in 13x9x2-inch casserole dish.
Mix all other ingredients together
and pour over broccoli.
Sprinkle top of casserole with
crushed cheese crackers.
Bake at 350º F for 30 minutes.

Serves 8

HONEY-BAKED ONIONS

6 medium sweet white onions
 (Vidalia, if available)
1 1/2 cups tomato juice
1 1/2 cups water
6 tsp honey
6 tsp butter, melted

Peel and trim onions. Cut in half and place in a buttered 13x9x2-inch baking dish.
Mix tomato juice, water, honey and butter in a small bowl.
Pour over onions.
Bake at 325° F for 1 hour, or until soft.

Makes 6 servings

They say the Earl of Sandwich gave birth to this idea. Well, in my house, my boys have the last word in this department. They can make a sandwich from almost anything, and they do so on a regular basis (and I mean regular). Which means keeping a supply of bread on hand is not always easy. And to top it off, sometimes you find it flattened in the grocery bag when you arrive home from the store. Lately, I have begun to buy flour tortillas, which are also available in low fat, or low carb. They are easy to store, take up no space and are already flat. They are great for making roll-up sandwiches. You can put almost anything in them and they are very transportable too. Keep some in the refrigerator for times when the bread supply runs out and the sandwich cravings don't.

Sandwiches

EGG SALAD SANDWICHES

5 large hard-boiled eggs, grated
2 tbsp sweet pickle relish
2 tbsp mayonnaise
1 tbsp sour cream
1/2 tsp Dijon mustard
1/4 tsp salt
1/4 tsp sugar
1/8 tsp ground black pepper
22 thin white sandwich bread slices

Combine first 8 ingredients in a bowl until blended.
Cover and chill 3 hours.
Spread 2 tablespoons egg mixture evenly on 1 side of 11 bread slices.
Top with remaining 11 bread slices.
Cut each sandwich into 4 finger sandwiches.

Makes 44 finger sandwiches

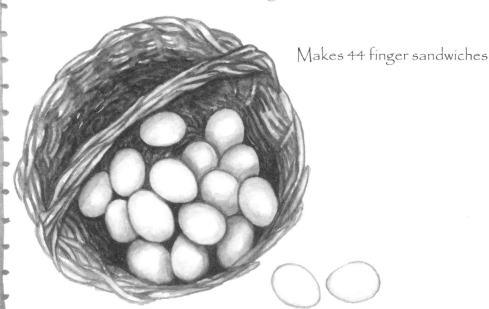

OPEN-FACED TURKEY SANDWICH
with APPLE

4 (2-oz.) slices country or peasant bread
4 tsp low-fat mayonnaise
4 tsp Dijon mustard
1 cup trimmed arugula
4 (1/8-inch-thick) slices red onion
2 oz. thinly sliced deli turkey
2 Fuji apples, each cored and cut crosswise into 8 (1/4-inch-thick) slices
1/2 cup (2oz.) grated Havarti cheese
Coarsely ground black pepper (optional)

Preheat broiler with oven rack in middle position.
Spread each bread slice with 1 tsp mayonnaise and 1 tsp mustard.
Layer each slice with 1/4 cup arugula, 1 onion slice, 3 ounces turkey,
4 apple slices and 2 tbsp cheese.
Place sandwiches on a baking sheet; broil 4 minutes or until cheese is
bubbly. Remove from oven; sprinkle with pepper, if desired. Serve
immediately.

Serves 4

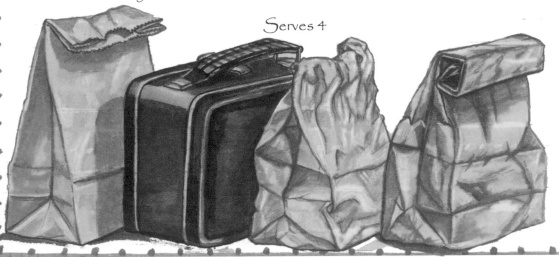

PEANUT BUTTER, APPLE and BACON SANDWICH

1/2 cup creamy or chunky peanut butter
4 large slices whole-wheat bread (each about 5 by 5 inches),
 toasted lightly
8 slices bacon, cooked until crisp and drained on paper towels
1 small crisp apple (such as Royal Gala), cored and sliced thin
1/2 cup alfalfa sprouts

Spread peanut butter evenly on bread slices.
Layer bacon, apple slices, and sprouts on 2 bread slices.
Top with remaining bread slices.

Serves 2

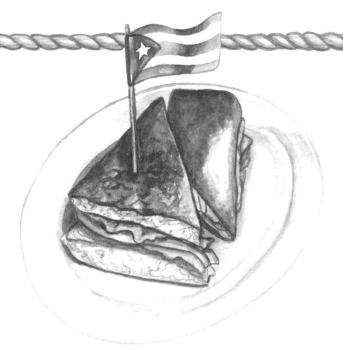

GRILLED CUBAN SANDWICHES

2 tbsp Dijon mustard
1 (8-oz.) loaf French bread, cut in half horizontally
6 oz. reduced-fat Swiss cheese, thinly sliced (such as Alpine Lace)
6 oz. deli-sliced ham (such as Hillshire Farms)
8 sandwich-sliced dill pickles
Cooking spray

Spread mustard evenly over cut sides of bread. Arrange half of cheese and half of ham on bottom half of loaf; top with pickle slices. Repeat layer with remaining cheese and ham; cover with top half of loaf.
Cut into quarters.
Heat a large, heavy skillet coated with cooking spray, over medium-high heat.
Add sandwiches; press with a heavy skillet (such as cast-iron).
Cook 2 minutes on each side.

Makes 4 servings

OPEN-FACED ROAST BEEF SANDWICHES

4 slices of Texas toast
8 slices roast beef
4 thick slices Swiss cheese
1 cup brown gravy

Place Texas toast on a cookie sheet and broil in oven until golden brown on both sides.
Remove from oven and place 2 slices of roast beef on each piece of toast, pour warm gravy over, then cover with Swiss cheese slice.
Return to oven just long enough to melt cheese.
Serve with mashed potatoes and tossed salad.

Makes 4 servings

You can serve lettuce and tomato on the side.

CALIFORNIA PITA

1 large pita, cut in half and opened
1 ripe avocado, peeled, pit removed, sliced
1 large ripe tomato, sliced
4 slices Swiss cheese
Leaf or Romaine lettuce leaves
Thousand Island dressing

Into each half of the pita, place
half the avocado, half the tomato,
2 slices of cheese, lettuce leaves
and dressing to your taste.

Makes 2 sandwiches

TURKEY PITA

8-inch white or wheat pita bread round
1/2 cup chopped cooked deli-roast turkey breast
1/2 cup prepared deli coleslaw
1 tbsp snipped, drained, oil-packed dried tomatoes

Slice pita in half and open. In each half, arrange turkey, coleslaw and
tomatoes. Serve with chips or pasta salad.

Makes 1 large sandwich

OPEN-FACED MONTE CRISTO

2 large eggs
1/2 cup milk
1/2 tsp salt
1/4 tsp pepper
4 (1-inch-thick) white bread
 slices
2 tbsp butter or margarine

4 tbsp strawberry jam or red currant
 jelly
4 oz. thinly sliced cooked turkey or
 chicken
4 oz. thinly sliced smoked cooked ham
8 (3/4-oz.) Swiss cheese slices
Powdered sugar (optional)

GARNISHES
Sliced whole strawberries, whole strawberries

Whisk together first 4 ingredients in a shallow dish. Dip both sides of
bread slices in egg mixture. Melt butter in a large skillet; add bread
slices, and cook 2 to 3 minutes on each side or until golden brown.
Spread 1 tbsp strawberry jam on 1 side of each bread slice; top evenly
with turkey, ham, and cheese. Place on a baking sheet.
Broil 5 inches from heat 2 to 3 minutes or until cheese is melted.
Sprinkle with powdered sugar, if desired. Garnish with strawberries, if
desired, and serve immediately.

Makes 4 servings

GOAT CHEESE and SALMON SANDWICHES

1/2 lb. soft mild goat cheese
  (such as Bucheron or Montrachet),
  room temperature
10 tbsp minced fresh arugula or
  watercress
5 tbsp olive oil
6 tsp minced fresh chives

Ground black pepper
1 lb. smoked salmon slices
2 tbsp fresh lemon juice
12 1/2-inch-thick egg bread slices
Fresh arugula or watercress leaves
12 thin lemon slices

Mix goat cheese, 6 tablespoons minced arugula, 2 tablespoons oil and 2 teaspoons chives in small bowl. Season generously with pepper. Arrange salmon in single layer on large plate. Drizzle 3 tablespoons oil over. Spoon lemon juice over. Sprinkle with 4 tablespoons minced arugula, 4 teaspoons chives and generous amount of pepper. (Can be prepared 4 hours ahead. Cover and refrigerate.) Just before serving, toast bread. Spread with goat cheese mixture; top with salmon. Place sandwiches on plates. Tuck arugula under sandwiches. Make cut in each lemon slice from center to edge. Twist 1 slice atop each sandwich.

SAY CHEESE

Makes 12 servings

In our household, main dish usually means LARGE dish. So I have scaled down some of these recipes from their original versions. I make lots of chicken dishes because they are inexpensive, and luckily enough everyone likes them. (The added benefit here is I had so much fun illustrating the chicken recipes!) Any dish with pasta is a hit in our home, as well. Hobo Dinner, a throwback from my childhood, is a great dish to have young cooks help you prepare. You can use chicken instead of the beef if you like. Ham and Egg Pie is another family favorite. My boys have been known to change their plans in order not to miss it. It also makes a great dish to serve for brunch. My son Zach makes the most awesome calzones. We think they rival any you might order in a restaurant. When he makes them, he puts the ingredients in bowls on the island, and each person fills a small dish with what they would like in theirs, and just hands it over to him to finish preparing. It is a real treat. You'll notice that I have listed two macaroni and cheese recipes and this says it all: it is, by far, the all-time dinner favorite.

Main Dishes

CRESCENT ROLL CHICKEN

1 medium onion, chopped
1/2 cup chopped celery
2 tbsp butter or margarine
3 cups chopped cooked chicken
1 can cream of mushroom soup
1 can cream of chicken soup
1 cup sour cream
1 can water chestnuts, drained
1 can refrigerated crescent rolls
1/2 stick margarine, melted

Sauté onion and celery in butter in a small skillet.
Transfer onion and celery to a large bowl. Add all other ingredients
except crescent rolls.
Mix until blended. Pour into a greased 13x9x2-inch casserole dish.
Unroll crescent rolls and place over the top of the chicken mixture;
brush with melted margarine. Bake at 325° F for 30 minutes.

Serves 6

BARBECUED CHICKEN

3 lbs. chicken, cut up
1/2 cup catsup
1/3 cup vinegar
1/4 cup brown sugar, packed
2 tsp margarine or butter
2 tbsp Worcestershire sauce
2 tbsp lemon juice
2 tsp salt
2 tsp chili powder
2 tsp prepared mustard
2 medium onions, sliced and separated into rings

Arrange chicken pieces in a 15x10x1-inch baking pan. Bake at 375º F
for 40 minutes; drain.
In the meantime, prepare sauce. In a saucepan, combine catsup, vinegar,
brown sugar, margarine, Worcestershire sauce, lemon juice, salt, chili
powder and mustard. Stir in onions.
Bring to boiling, reduce heat, and simmer, uncovered, for 10 minutes.
Turn chicken pieces and baste with sauce.
Bake 10 minutes more or until tender.

Makes 8 to 10 servings

CHICKEN and DRESSING

3 chicken breast halves
Water
1/4 tsp salt
4 cups cornbread crumbs
1 cup biscuit or bread crumbs
1 medium onion, chopped

4 ribs celery, chopped
1 1/2 tsp ground sage
Salt and pepper to taste
3 eggs, beaten
1/4 to 1/2 cup margarine, melted
Cooking spray

In a large pot, cover chicken with cold water and add salt. Bring to boiling, lower heat to medium; cook 1 to 1 1/2 hours until fork tender. Remove chicken to cool; reserve broth. Remove chicken meat from bone and chop; set aside.

Put both bread crumbs in a large mixing bowl; add onion, celery, sage, salt and pepper.

Pour enough reserved broth over mixture to moisten well. Stir in eggs and margarine; mix well. Add chopped chicken.

Spray a 13x9x2-inch baking dish with cooking spray. Pour chicken mixture into pan.

Bake at 350º F for 45 minutes.

Serves 8 to 10

EASY CHICKEN PIE

2 cups chopped cooked chicken
5 hard-boiled eggs
1 cup chicken broth
1 can cream of chicken soup
1 cup of biscuit mix
1/3 cup milk
1 stick of butter or margarine, melted

In a baking dish, layer chicken and eggs. Mix broth and soup; pour over layers.
Mix biscuit mix with milk; pour over all.
Drizzle with melted butter.
Bake at 350º F for 40 minutes or until golden brown.

Serves 6

HOT CHICKEN SALAD

1 whole chicken, cooked and chopped
1 1/2 cups chopped celery
1 cup mayonnaise
1 can cream of chicken soup
1 small onion, chopped
2 cups crumbled saltine crackers

Mix first five ingredients in a large bowl.
Pour into a 13x9x2-inch baking dish.
Cover with crackers. Bake at 375º F for 30 minutes.

Serves 4 to 6

THANKSGIVING TURKEY

NOTE:

I am from the South. Which means that I was brought up never having eaten a 'stuffed turkey'. We serve ours with dressing in a pan separate from the bird.

TURKEY

1 fresh turkey
1 purchased roasting bag, large
2 tbsp flour
1 large onion, peeled, cut in 4 pieces

Remove the gizzard, liver, etc. from inside the turkey, discard. Rinse turkey and pat dry. Open the cooking bag and put about 2 tbsp flour inside. Shake.
Add the turkey, and the onion. Close bag and place in a roasting pan.

Cook according to weight:
8 lbs. to 12 lbs. - 1 1/2 to 2 hours
12 lbs. to 16 lbs. - 2 1/2 hours
16 lbs. to 20 lbs. - 3 hours
20 lbs. to 24 lbs. - 4 hours

Watch the Macy's Parade while you wait.

DRESSING

1 lb. sage-flavored sausage, sliced
4 cups cornbread crumbs
1 cup biscuit or bread crumbs
1 medium onion, chopped
4 ribs celery, chopped
1 1/2 tsp ground sage
Salt and pepper to taste
Chicken broth
Water
3 eggs, beaten
1/4 to 1/2 cup margarine, melted
Cooking spray

Cook sausage in a large skillet, drain and set aside.
Put both bread crumbs in a large mixing bowl; add sausage, onion, celery, sage, salt and pepper.
Pour enough broth and water over mixture to moisten very well. Stir in eggs and margarine; mix well. Spray a 13x9x2-inch baking dish with cooking spray. Pour mixture into pan. Bake at 350º F for 45 minutes.

Serves 8 to 10

SOUTHERN FRIED CHICKEN

6 chicken breast halves, boneless and skinless
2 eggs, beaten
1 cup milk
2 cups flour
1 tsp salt
1/2 tsp pepper
Vegetable oil for frying

Wash chicken breasts and pat dry.
Mix eggs and milk in a small bowl. Mix flour and salt and pepper in another small bowl.
Heat oil in an electric skillet at 350° F.
Dip chicken in egg mixture then into flour mixture; repeat.
Place in the hot oil and cook until brown and crisp on both sides, turning once, about 7 to 10 minutes per side. Drain on plate covered in paper towels.
Serve with a jar of purchased chicken gravy, if you like.

Serves 6

LEMON BAKED CHICKEN

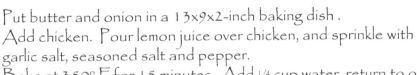

1 stick butter or margarine, melted
1 small onion, diced
6 chicken breasts, skinned
1/2 cup lemon juice
1/4 tsp garlic salt
Dash seasoned salt
Dash of pepper
1/4 cup water

Put butter and onion in a 13x9x2-inch baking dish .
Add chicken. Pour lemon juice over chicken, and sprinkle with
garlic salt, seasoned salt and pepper.
Bake at 350° F for 15 minutes. Add 1/4 cup water, return to oven, cook
for 50 minutes more or until tender.

Makes 6 servings

CHICKEN and RICE CASSEROLE

1 stick margarine
Salt and pepper
1 chicken, cut up
1 can cream of celery soup

1 can cream of chicken soup
2 cups water
2 cups rice, uncooked

Melt margarine. Salt and pepper chicken pieces and dip into melted
margarine; set aside. In a 2-quart greased casserole dish, mix the soups,
water and remaining margarine. Mix well so there are no lumps.
Add rice. Place the chicken pieces on top. Cook at 350° F for 1 hour.

Serves 6

WHITE CHILI

1 medium onion, finely chopped
3 tbsp olive oil
4-oz. can green chilies, drained
3 tbsp all-purpose flour
2 tsp ground cumin
3 15-oz. cans great northern beans
1 can chicken broth
1 1/2 cups finely chopped cooked chicken breast
Shredded Monterey Jack cheese
Sour cream

In a large skillet, cook onion in oil for 4 minutes or until clear.
Add chilies, flour and cumin. Cook and stir for 2 minutes.
Pour 1 can of beans into a blender or food processor, process until smooth.
Add beans, bean purée and chicken broth to the skillet with the onions; bring to boiling.
Reduce heat and simmer for 10 minutes.
Add chicken; cook until hot.
At serving, garnish with shredded cheese and sour cream.

Makes 6 servings

PARMESAN CHICKEN with LEMON BUTTER PASTA

1/2 cup grated Parmesan cheese
1/4 cup dry bread crumbs
1 tsp dried oregano
1 tsp dried parsley flakes
1/4 tsp paprika
1/4 tsp salt
1/4 tsp pepper
6 chicken breast halves, boneless and skinless
1/4 cup butter or margarine, melted
1 box of dry linguine
Salt
1/2 cup butter or margarine, melted
1 tbsp minced garlic
4 tbsp lemon juice
1/2 cup Parmesan cheese
1/4 cup chopped fresh parsley

In a large bowl, combine the first seven ingredients. Dip chicken in butter and then into the crumb mixture. Place in a greased 13x9x2-inch baking pan. Bake at 400º F for 20 to 25 minutes or until chicken is tender and when pierced, juices run clear. In a large pot, cook pasta in salted water until tender, about 8 to 10 minutes. In a small saucepan, mix butter, garlic and lemon juice; stir over medium heat until heated through. Toss with pasta until coated. Place on a serving dish and sprinkle with Parmesan cheese. Place chicken breasts on top and sprinkle with fresh parsley.

Serves 6

CUBED STEAK and GRAVY

2 cups flour
1 tbsp salt
1 tsp pepper
8 pieces of cubed steak
Oil for browning
3 tbsp flour
3 beef bouillon cubes
2 cups plus hot water

In a large bowl, mix flour with salt and pepper.
Dredge steak pieces in flour mixture.
In the meantime, pour enough oil to totally cover the bottom of pan to about 1/2-inch; heat oil over medium heat.
Brown each piece of steak, turning once. Remove pieces to drain on paper towels.
When all steaks are browned and removed, sprinkle 3 tbsp flour and bouillon cubes, crushed into dripping from steaks.
Stir until dissolved.
Add water and simmer until slightly thickened. If it becomes too thick, add more water; stir.
Return steak to pan and simmer for 10 minutes.
Serve over mashed potatoes or rice.

Serves 8

BARBEQUED SPARE RIBS

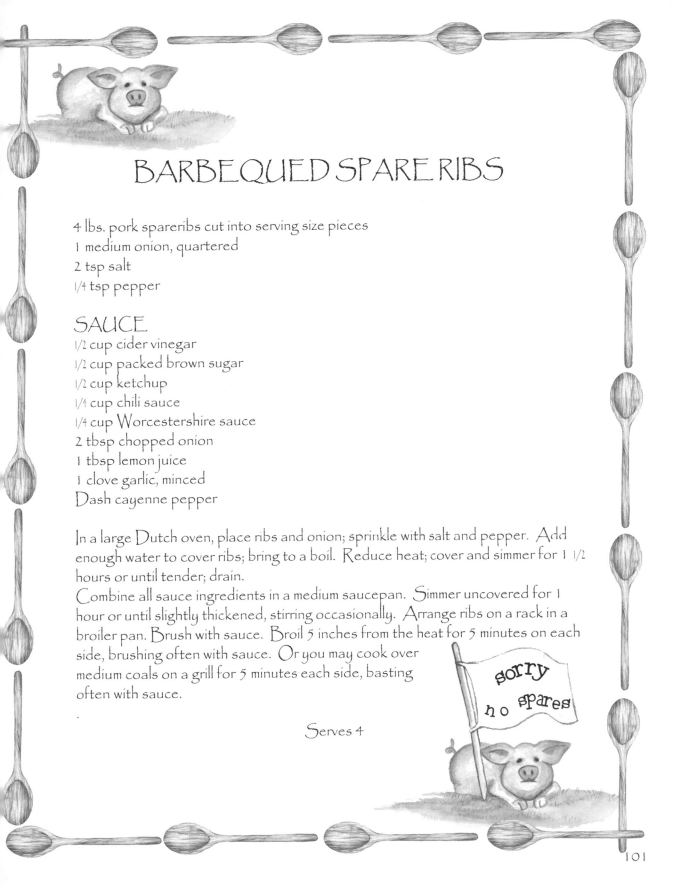

4 lbs. pork spareribs cut into serving size pieces
1 medium onion, quartered
2 tsp salt
1/4 tsp pepper

SAUCE
1/2 cup cider vinegar
1/2 cup packed brown sugar
1/2 cup ketchup
1/4 cup chili sauce
1/4 cup Worcestershire sauce
2 tbsp chopped onion
1 tbsp lemon juice
1 clove garlic, minced
Dash cayenne pepper

In a large Dutch oven, place ribs and onion; sprinkle with salt and pepper. Add enough water to cover ribs; bring to a boil. Reduce heat; cover and simmer for 1 1/2 hours or until tender; drain.
Combine all sauce ingredients in a medium saucepan. Simmer uncovered for 1 hour or until slightly thickened, stirring occasionally. Arrange ribs on a rack in a broiler pan. Brush with sauce. Broil 5 inches from the heat for 5 minutes on each side, brushing often with sauce. Or you may cook over medium coals on a grill for 5 minutes each side, basting often with sauce.

Serves 4

sorry no spares

CHEESEBURGER PIE

1 lb. lean ground beef
1 1/2 cups chopped onion
1/2 tsp salt
1/4 tsp pepper
1 cup shredded Cheddar cheese
1 1/2 cups milk
3/4 cup Jiffy baking mix
3 eggs

Lightly grease a 10-inch pie plate.
In a large skillet, cook beef and onion until beef is browned and onion is clear. Drain. Add salt and pepper.
Spread beef in pie plate and sprinkle with cheese.
In a medium bowl, beat together remaining ingredients.
Pour over beef.
Bake at 400º F for 30 minutes or until golden brown.
Let stand 5 minutes before cutting into pie pieces.

Serves 6

HOBO DINNER

2 lbs. lean ground beef
6 large potatoes
2 medium onions
1 lb. baby, or sliced carrots
1/2 stick margarine
Salt and pepper

Shape ground beef into patties. Peel potatoes and chop into large chunks.
Peel onions and cut into quarters.
Take aluminum foil, three times as much as the surface of the pan, and center
over pan, with excess on each side.
Place beef in center, potatoes on one side and carrots and onions on the
other.
Season with salt and pepper, and dot with margarine.
Cover with excess aluminum foil. Cook at 400° F for 1 hour.

Makes 8 servings

All-time
family
favorite!

BEEF STROGANOFF

2 lbs. steak, (any cut you prefer)
1/8 lb. butter
1 large can mushrooms, sliced
1/8 lb. butter
1 large onion, diced
1/2 can beef consommé
1 tbsp vinegar
1/2 pint sour cream
Salt and pepper to taste
Egg noodles, cooked

Cut steak into strips and sauté in butter in a medium skillet.
In a small skillet, sauté mushrooms in butter; add onions and cook until onions are clear.
Add mushrooms and onions to the steak. Add consommé, vinegar and sour cream; season with salt and pepper.
Bring to a boil, lower heat and simmer 30 minutes. Serve over cooked egg noodles.

Makes 6 servings

BUSY WOMAN MEATLOAF

1 lb. lean ground beef
1 envelope dry onion soup mix
1 egg, beaten
1 small can evaporated milk
Salt and pepper to taste
1/2 cup catsup

Mix all ingredients together, except catsup, and shape into a loaf.
Cook in a shallow 1 1/2-quart baking dish at 350º F for 1 hour.
Remove from oven, spread catsup over top.

Serves 4

SPECIAL MEATLOAF

1 cup sour cream
2 green onions, sliced
4 12-oz. cans sliced mushrooms, drained
2 tsp salt
2 lbs. ground beef
1 1/2 tbsp Worcestershire sauce
2 eggs
1/3 cup milk

Preheat oven to 350º F. In a small bowl, mix sour cream, onions and
mushrooms. Set aside. Combine remaining ingredients in a medium
bowl; mix well. Shape in a long 4-inch wide rectangle, and place in an
ungreased shallow baking dish. Make a 2-inch wide indention down
the middle of the loaf; spoon sour cream mixture into the indention.
Bake one hour. Let stand 10 minutes before slicing.

Serves 6

HAM and EGG CASSEROLE

6 hard-boiled eggs
1/4 cup finely chopped celery
1 tbsp mayonnaise
1 tsp prepared mustard
6 slices cooked ham
1 can cream of mushroom soup
1/3 cup milk
1/4 cup crushed potato chips
½ cup grated Cheddar cheese

Slice eggs in half and remove yolks. In a small bowl, mash yolks, combine with celery, mayonnaise and mustard.
Refill whites with yolk mixture, and put the halves back together.
Wrap each egg with a ham slice and place, fold side down in a 9x9-inch baking dish.
In a small bowl, mix together soup and milk. Pour over eggs, top with chips and cheese.
Bake at 350º F for 30 minutes.

Serves 6

SHEPHERD'S PIE

2 cups cooked chopped meat
2 cups gravy
1 tbsp finely chopped onion
Salt and pepper
2 cups mashed potatoes, prepared with milk and seasonings, as desired
1 tbsp butter
1/8 tsp paprika

Combine meat, gravy, and chopped onion; season with salt and pepper to taste.
Line the bottom of a buttered baking dish with a layer of half of the seasoned mashed potatoes.
Add meat mixture, then cover with remaining mashed potatoes. Or, meat and gravy can be put in the baking dish first then topped with all of the mashed potatoes.
Dot mashed potato topping with butter, sprinkle with salt, pepper, and paprika, then bake for about 30 minutes at 400° F, or until potato topping is browned and the pie is thoroughly heated.

Serves 4

SWEDISH MEATBALLS

1 1/2 lbs. lean ground beef
1 envelope dry onion soup mix
1 egg, beaten
Ground black pepper
2 tsp Worcestershire sauce
2 cans cream of mushroom soup
1 cup milk

Mix together ground beef, onion soup mix, egg, pepper and
Worcestershire sauce until mixture holds together. Form small meatballs
and cook in a large skillet, seasoned with cooking spray, until browned on
all sides. Drain on paper towels.
Mix together soup and milk until smooth; pour into a 2-quart casserole
dish. Add meatballs and bake at 350° F for 30 minutes. Serve over
cooked rice or noodles.

Serves 4 to 6

PORCUPINE BEEF BALLS

1/2 cup uncooked rice
1 lb. lean ground beef
1 1/4 tsp salt
1/4 tsp pepper
2 cans crushed tomatoes
3 tbsp butter or margarine
2 tbsp chopped green pepper
3 tbsp chopped onion
2 tbsp all-purpose flour

Combine rice, ground beef, salt, pepper and
1/4 cup of the tomatoes. Mix and form into
twelve meatballs. Place in a 3-quart casserole
dish.
Melt butter or margarine in a skillet. Add green
pepper and onion and brown lightly.
Blend in flour and slowly add remaining tomatoes;
cook until thickened.
Pour over meatballs, cover and bake at 375º F for
1 1/2 hours.

Serves 6

I don't volunteer

HAMBURGER PIE

1 lb. lean ground beef
1 onion, chopped
1 can tomato soup
1 can whole kernel corn
1 can baby English peas
3 cups mashed potatoes

In a medium cast-iron skillet, cook beef with onion until beef is browned and onion is transparent. Drain.
Add tomato soup and simmer 20 minutes.
Add corn and peas and simmer 15 minutes longer.
Top with mashed potatoes and put skillet in oven on broil just until potatoes are slightly browned.

Serves 4

HAM and EGG PIE

2 cups chopped cooked ham
5 hard-boiled eggs, chopped
1 cup milk
1 can cream of mushroom soup
1 1/2 cups biscuit mix
1 cup milk
1 stick margarine, melted

Layer ham and eggs in a 13x9x2-inch baking dish. Mix milk and soup; pour over all. Mix biscuit mix with milk; pour over all.

Drizzle melted margarine over top. Bake at 350º F for 40 minutes or until bubbly and golden brown on top.

Serves 6 to 8

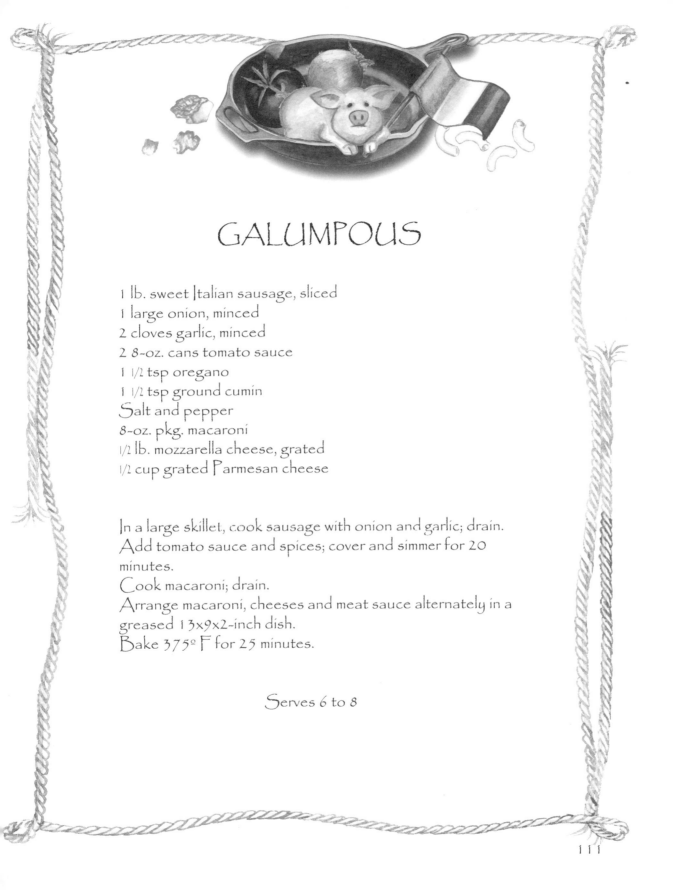

GALUMPOUS

1 lb. sweet Italian sausage, sliced
1 large onion, minced
2 cloves garlic, minced
2 8-oz. cans tomato sauce
1 1/2 tsp oregano
1 1/2 tsp ground cumin
Salt and pepper
8-oz. pkg. macaroni
1/2 lb. mozzarella cheese, grated
1/2 cup grated Parmesan cheese

In a large skillet, cook sausage with onion and garlic; drain.
Add tomato sauce and spices; cover and simmer for 20
minutes.
Cook macaroni; drain.
Arrange macaroni, cheeses and meat sauce alternately in a
greased 13x9x2-inch dish.
Bake 375º F for 25 minutes.

Serves 6 to 8

this one takes no time!

JOHNNY MASUKI

1 lb. lean ground beef
4 medium onions, chopped
1 green pepper, chopped
1 clove garlic, chopped
2 tbsp chili powder
1 tbsp Worcestershire
1 small can pimento
1 can tomato soup
1 cup water
1 pkg. broad egg noodles
1 cup grated smoked Gouda cheese

In a large skillet, cook beef and onions; drain.
Add all other ingredients, bring to boiling, reduce heat, cover and simmer for 15 minutes.
In the meantime, cook noodles according to package directions; drain.
Pour beef mixture over noodles in a large casserole, and top with grated cheese.

Makes 6 to 8 servings

PORK LOIN ROAST with SWEET POTATO STUFFED APPLES

1 pork loin roast
Salt and pepper to taste
1 tsp sage
6 or 8 large tart baking apples
1 6-oz. can sweet potatoes or yams
1/4 cup brown sugar
1 tsp salt
1 tsp cinnamon
1/2 cup slivered almonds
1/4 cup melted butter
1/4 cup maple syrup

Rub roast with 1/2 tsp salt per pound. Sprinkle with pepper and sage. Place roast, with the fat side up, on a roasting rack in an open roasting pan. Do not add water.
Roast in a 300º F oven for 4 hours, or until done.
In the meantime, core apples. Remove pulp, enough to make a 1 1/2-inch opening in each apple.
In a medium bowl, mash potatoes with apple pulp (be sure there are no seeds), brown sugar, salt, cinnamon, and half the almonds.
Blend butter and syrup in a small saucepan; heat through. Spoon 1 tsp syrup mixture into each apple. Spoon sweet potato mixture into each apple and top with remaining almonds.
Place apples in a buttered baking dish and bake at 300º F for 1 hour; baste occasionally with remaining syrup mixture.
At serving, place roast on large serving platter and surround with stuffed apples.

Serves 6 to 8

PASTICCIO

8 oz. fusilli, or any short pasta
1 tbsp olive oil
4 tbsp heavy cream

SAUCE
2 tbsp olive oil, plus
1 medium onion, thinly sliced
1 red bell pepper, deseeded and chopped
2 garlic cloves, chopped
1 lb. lean ground beef
14-oz. can chopped tomatoes
1/2 cup dry white wine
2 tbsp chopped fresh parsley
Salt and pepper to taste

TOPPING
1 1/4 cups plain yogurt
3 eggs
Pinch of grated nutmeg
1/2 cup grated Parmesan cheese

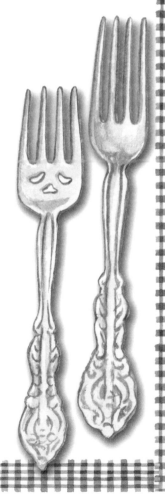

Cook pasta in salted water with 1 tbsp olive oil, for 8-10 minutes, or until tender. Drain and transfer to bowl.
For the sauce: heat the oil in a large skillet and cook the onion and red bell pepper for 3 minutes.
Stir in the garlic and cook for 1 minute more. Stir in beef and cook, stirring often, until browned.
Add tomatoes and wine; bring to boiling. Reduce heat and simmer for 20 minutes.
Stir in parsley and salt and pepper to taste.
Stir cream into the cooked pasta.

TOPPING

Beat together the yogurt, eggs and nutmeg until well blended and season with salt and pepper.

Grease a 13x9x2-inch baking dish. Spoon in half the pasta and cover with half the sauce.

Repeat layers, then spread topping evenly as final layer and sprinkle lastly with Parmesan cheese.

Bake at 375º F for 25 minutes, or until topping is golden brown.

Serves 6

JOHNSON GRAVY

1 can Spam
3 tbsp shortening
2 tbsp flour
2 cups milk
4 hard-boiled eggs, chopped
Salt and pepper to taste

Chop Spam into small cubes and brown in shortening. Add flour and blend well; add milk, stirring constantly. When thickened, add chopped eggs and salt and pepper to taste.
Serve over biscuits.

Serves 6

gotta have biscuits

SAUSAGE GRAVY

2 lbs. ground pork sausage, mild or spicy
4 tbsp flour
2 cups half-and-half
1/2 cup skim milk or water

In a large skillet, brown sausage over medium heat. Stir in flour until dissolved. Slowly add the half-and-half stirring constantly until thickened. Add skim milk or water and cook until desired thickness is achieved. Serve over biscuits sliced in half.

Serves 6

My roast belongs to mama.

MAMA JOHNSON'S ROAST BEEF

4-lb. boneless beef roast
Salt and pepper to taste
Shortening for browning
Hot water

Salt and pepper roast. In a large cast-iron skillet, heat 3 tablespoons of shortening.
Brown meat on all sides, turning it as it browns.
Place meat in a roasting pan with a lid. Pour hot water over roast, enough to cover. Bring to a boil; turn down heat to medium-low. Cook, on stove top, very slowly for 4 to 5 hours. Check occasionally to make sure liquid does not boil away; add more if needed.

Serves 6

CHILI

2 lbs. lean ground beef
1 large onion, chopped
3 tbsp chili powder
2 tsp salt

2 cans chicken broth
1 tsp sugar
2 large cans crushed tomatoes
2 cans chili hot beans, undrained

Cook beef and onion in a large skillet until beef is browned and onion is clear; drain. Add chili powder and salt. In a large soup pot, combine broth, sugar and tomatoes. Heat to boiling; add beef and beans. Return to boiling, and then reduce heat.
Simmer, covered, about 20 minutes.

Serves 6

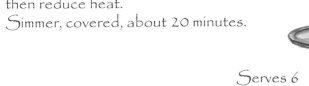

SAUSAGE and ONION BAKE

1 lb. sausage, sliced
2 large sweet onions, chopped
1 can cream of chicken soup
1 cup grated sharp Cheddar cheese
1 large jar mushrooms, sliced
3 cups bread crumbs
1/2 cup melted butter or margarine

In a medium skillet, cook sausage and onions until done; drain.
In a large bowl, mix sausage and onions with all other ingredients, except
bread crumbs and butter.
Pour mixture into a greased 13x9x2-inch baking dish.
Mix bread crumbs with butter; spread over all.
Cover lightly with foil and bake at 350º F for 20 minutes. Remove foil and
bake another 10 to 15 minutes, or until golden brown.

Serves 6

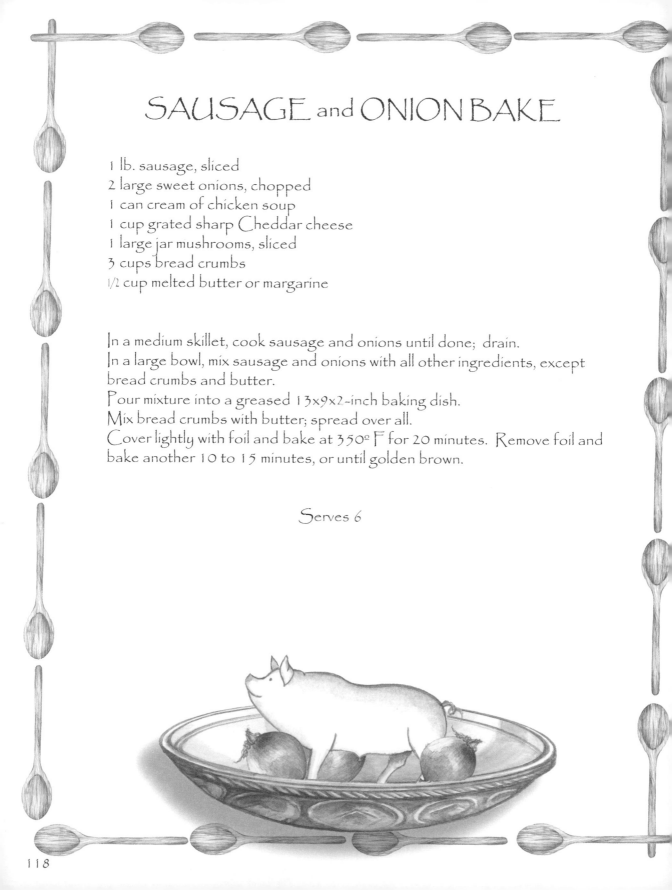

ZACH'S CALZONES

4 cans Pillsbury Pizza Crust
Flour
8 tbsp pesto sauce, fresh or canned
16-oz. container ricotta cheese
3 cups shredded mozzarella cheese
1 cup grated Parmesan cheese
Non-stick cooking spray
1 large jar marinara sauce

Assorted toppings of your choice:
Fresh spinach leaves
Ground sausage or ground beef, cooked
Pepperoni slices
Mushrooms
Chopped chicken, cooked

Use one can of crust for each calzone. For each: open can and spread dough out on a floured chopping board to form a circle.
Spread 2 tbsp of pesto sauce over surface of half of each circle.
Add cheeses and top with toppings of your choice. Fold over and crimp edges with your fingers until sealed.
Spray a cookie sheet with non-stick cooking spray and carefully place calzones on the pan. Pierce top of crust with a fork once.
Bake at 375º F on top shelf of oven until golden brown.
Allow to cool slightly   before cutting in half to serve.
Serve heated marinara   sauce on the side.

Each calzone serves 2,
8 servings total

EASY ENCHILADAS

1 lb. lean ground beef
1 medium onion, chopped
1 6-oz. carton of cottage cheese
1 2-pack of flour tortillas
1 large jar of picante sauce
1 large jar of salsa
2 cups grated Monterey Jack cheese

In a large skillet, cook ground beef and onion until beef is browned and onion is clear; drain.
In a large bowl, mix beef and onion with cottage cheese.
Spread a portion of beef and cheese mixture on each tortilla and roll up. Place rolled tortillas, seam side down in a greased 13x9x2-inch baking dish.
In a small bowl, mix together picante sauce and salsa.
Pour over enchiladas and sprinkle with grated cheese.
Bake at 350° F for 25 minutes.

Serves 6 to 8

MEXICAN LASAGNA

2 lbs. ground beef
1 large onion, chopped
1 large jar picante sauce
1 large jar salsa
16-oz. carton cottage cheese
2 eggs beaten
3 cups grated cheese, Monterey Jack or Cheddar
2 pkg. 8-inch corn tortillas

In a large skillet, cook beef and onions until done; drain. Add picante sauce and salsa and simmer 10 minutes.
In a medium bowl, mix cottage cheese with eggs; stir until blended.
In a 13x9x2-inch baking dish, place tortillas evenly, enough to cover the bottom of the dish. Next pour half of the sauce, spreading evenly, then the cottage cheese and 1 cup of the grated cheese. Continue layering ending with sauce on top, sprinkled with the remaining cheese.
Bake at 350º F for 30 minutes.

Serves 8

CURRIED SHRIMP

1 can cream of chicken soup
1/4 cup milk
1 lb. of shrimp, cooked and drained
2 tsp curry powder
3 cups cooked rice, hot
1/4 cup chopped fresh Italian parsley
3 tbsp butter

Blend soup with milk in a medium saucepan.
Add shrimp and curry powder; heat through.
In a large serving bowl, mix rice with parsley and butter.
Pour curried shrimp over all.
Serve immediately.

Makes 4 servings

MUSHROOM SHRIMP CREOLE

6 slices bacon
3 medium onions, chopped
4 celery ribs, chopped
2 medium bell peppers, chopped
2 6-oz. cans tomatoes or 12 fresh ripe tomatoes, peeled
1 tbsp oregano
1 tsp thyme
Dash hot sauce
Salt and pepper to taste
1 doz. fresh large mushrooms, sliced, or 2 cans sliced
 mushrooms
3 lbs. shrimp (boiled, peeled and deveined)
Cooked rice

In a large skillet, fry bacon until crisp and remove.
Sauté onions, celery and peppers in bacon
drippings until tender.
Mash tomatoes with their juices and add to pan.
Add remaining seasonings.
Cook for 1 hour on low, stirring often.
Add mushrooms, and cook for another
30 minutes.
In a large serving bowl, add shrimp to sauce
when ready to serve.
Serve with rice.

Makes 8 to 10 servings

CATALINA SALMON QUICHE

2 3-oz. pkg. cream cheese, softened
1/2 cup dairy sour cream
2 eggs
2 tbsp prepared mustard
7 3/4-oz. can salmon, drained and chopped
1 frozen 9-inch deep pie crust
1 pkg. frozen chopped broccoli, thawed and drained
1/4 cup shredded Swiss cheese
1/4 cup chopped pitted ripe olives

Using mixer or blender, combine cream cheese, sour cream, eggs and mustard until well blended.
Arrange chopped salmon in bottom of unbaked pie crust; add broccoli.
Pour cream cheese mixture over salmon and broccoli.
Sprinkle with cheese and olives.
Bake at 375° F for 40 to 45 minutes, or until a knife inserted in center comes out clean.
Serve warm or cold.

Serves 8

CRAB CASSEROLE

1 medium onion, chopped
2 stalks celery, chopped
1/2 stick margarine
1 lb. crabmeat
1 tbsp flour
4 slices bread, torn into small pieces
4 hard-boiled eggs, grated
1 tbsp Worcestershire sauce
Dash hot sauce
1 tbsp vinegar
Salt and pepper to taste
1/4 cup evaporated milk
2 tbsp prepared mustard
2 tbsp catsup
2/3 cup bread crumbs
1/8 cup margarine or butter, melted

Saute onion and celery in margarine. Transfer to a large bowl.
Mix together all other ingredients, except bread crumbs and margarine.
Pour into a greased 13x9x2-inch casserole dish.
Mix bread crumbs with melted margarine; sprinkle over crabmeat mixture to cover.
Bake at 350º F for 30 minutes.

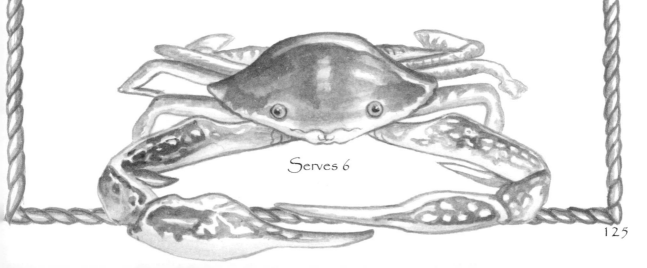

Serves 6

GRILLED SALMON

4 salmon fillets
1/2 cup virgin olive oil
1/2 cup lemon juice
4 green onions, thinly sliced
3 tbsp minced fresh parsley
1 1/2 tsp minced fresh rosemary
1/2 tsp salt
1/2 tsp pepper

Place the salmon fillets in a greased 13x9x2-inch
baking dish. Combine remaining ingredients and
mix well. Set aside 1/4 cup of mixture for basting;
pour the rest over the salmon. Cover and
refrigerate for 30 minutes.
Drain salmon, discarding the liquid.
Grill salmon over medium coals, skin-side down,
for 15 to 20 minutes, or until fish flakes easily
with a fork. Baste occasionally with
reserved marinade.

Makes 4 servings

BAKED TILAPIA with SHRIMP SAUCE

Non-stick cooking spray
8 tilapia fillets
Salt and pepper to taste
1/4 cup butter or margarine, melted
1/2 cup grated Parmesan cheese
2 jars Alfredo sauce
1 lb. small salad shrimp, cooked, drained and deveined
3 tbsp chopped fresh Italian parsley

On a foil-lined baking sheet with edges, spray non-stick cooking spray.
Place fillets and season with salt and pepper. Drizzle butter over, and then sprinkle with Parmesan cheese. Bake in 350º F oven for 10 to 12 minutes, or until fish flakes easily with a fork.
In a small saucepan, pour the Alfredo sauce and heat through. Just before serving, add shrimp, stir until warmed.
Arrange fillets on a serving platter and pour sauce over evenly and sprinkle with parsley.

Serves 8

CRAB and SHRIMP CASSEROLE

1 1/2 cups cooked shrimp, chopped
1 cup chopped celery
1 cup crabmeat
3/4 cup mayonnaise
1/2 cup finely chopped green pepper
1/2 cup finely chopped onion
1 tsp Worcestershire sauce
1 tsp salt
1/4 tsp pepper
1 cup seasoned bread crumbs
1/2 cup melted butter

Combine all ingredients in a large bowl, except bread crumbs and butter. Pour into a 13x9x2-inch baking dish.
In a small bowl, mix bread crumbs and butter; spread over the top.
Bake at 350º F for 35 to 40 minutes.

Serves 6

FRIED CATFISH

6 catfish fillets
2 cups milk
2 cups yellow cornmeal mix
1 tbsp seasoned salt
2 tsp pepper
1/2 tsp onion powder
1/2 tsp garlic powder
1 tsp salt
Oil for frying

Place fillets in a shallow dish in a single layer. Cover with milk and chill in the refrigerator for at least one hour.

Mix cornmeal, seasoned salt, pepper, onion powder and garlic powder in a shallow bowl or dish.

Remove fillets from the refrigerator and let them warm up to room temperature (about 10 minutes). Remove fillets from milk and sprinkle with salt; discard milk.

Dredge catfish fillets in cornmeal mixture.

Pour oil 1 1/2 inches deep into a large electric skillet; heat to 350º F.

Fry fillets about 3 to 4 minutes on each side until golden brown.

Drain on paper towels.

Makes 6 servings

SALMON-STUFFED TOMATOES

1 5-oz. can salmon
1/3 cup sliced green onions
1/3 cup chopped celery
2 1/4-oz. can pitted ripe olives, drained and sliced
6 large tomatoes
Salt and pepper to taste
2/3 cup sour cream
Romaine lettuce leaves
2 medium cucumbers, sliced thin

Drain, bone, skin and flake salmon. In a medium bowl, mix salmon with onions, celery and olives. Place in refrigerator, covered, for 1 hour.
Cut off top from each tomato. Scoop out center to form a cup; drain upside down. Chill tomatoes. Sprinkle the inside of tomatoes with salt and pepper.
Fold sour cream into salmon mixture, salt and pepper to taste. Spoon into tomato cups.
Arrange lettuce leaves and cucumbers on a large serving platter; place tomatoes on top to serve.

Serves 6

FISH TACOS

6 fresh tilapia fillets
1 cup fish breading for frying
Salt and pepper
Non-stick cooking spray
6 large flour tortillas
2 cups chopped lettuce
2 large tomatoes, chopped
1 1/2 cups shredded Monterey Jack cheese
1 bottle Thousand Island dressing

Rinse tilapia fillets. In a large bowl, mix fish breading mix with salt and pepper.
Cover a cookie sheet with aluminum foil and spray well with cooking spray.
Dredge fillets in breading mix and place on foil-lined pan.
Spray fillets with the cooking spray until they no longer look dry.
Cook in a 350º F oven for 6 minutes, turn fillets, and cook another 5 to 7 minutes, or until fillets flake easily with a fork.
Into each flour tortilla, place 1 piece of fish, and equal amounts of lettuce, tomato and cheese; top each with dressing. Fold over tortilla.

Serves 6 to 8 depending on fillet size

PENNE PASTA with FRESH TOMATOES

1 lb. penne pasta
8 fresh ripe plum tomatoes, chopped
1/4 cup chopped fresh basil leaves
2 tbsp minced onion
1/2 cup Italian salad dressing, (low fat is OK)
1/2 cup grated Parmesan cheese

Cook pasta according to package directions; drain and set aside.
In a large bowl, combine all other ingredients, except cheese.
Add cooked pasta and toss till coated. Add cheese and stir until coated.

Makes 8 servings

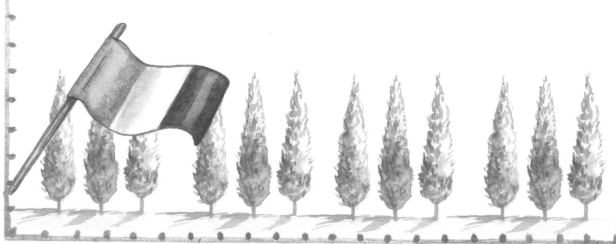

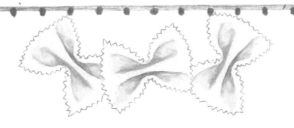

PASTA with NUTS and CHEESE

1 cup pine nuts
12 oz. bowtie pasta
2 zucchini squash, sliced
1 1/4 cups broccoli florets
1 cup Havarti cheese, cubed
2/3 cup milk
4 1/2 oz. white mushrooms, sliced
1 tbsp chopped fresh basil
3 oz. blue cheese, crumbled
Salt and pepper

Toast pine nuts on a cookie sheet on broil, turning occasionally until lightly browned.
Cook the pasta in salted water for 8-10 minutes or until tender, but firm; drain.
In the meantime, in a medium saucepan, cook zucchini and broccoli in a small amount of boiling, salted water for about 5 minutes or until just tender; drain.
Put the cheese into a pan with the milk and heat slowly on low to medium heat, stirring often.
Add the basil and mushrooms and cook for 3 minutes.
Stir in blue cheese and salt and pepper to taste.
In a large serving bowl, mix the pasta with the vegetables and add pine nuts.
Pour sauce over all and toss gently to mix.

Makes 4 servings

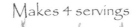

CLASSIC MACARONI and CHEESE

16-oz. box elbow macaroni
Salt and pepper to taste
1 1/2 cups shredded Cheddar cheese
6 eggs
2 tsp flour
1 cup milk

Cook macaroni according to package directions; drain.
Butter a 13x9x2-inch baking dish. Salt and pepper macaroni to taste and add to dish.
Cover macaroni with shredded cheese.
Beat eggs, flour and milk together; pour over cheese and macaroni. If needed, add more milk until macaroni is covered.
Bake at 350º F for 40 minutes.

Serves 8

EASY MACARONI and CHEESE

8 oz. large elbow macaroni, cooked and drained

8-oz. pkg. shredded sharp Cheddar cheese

10 3/4-oz. can cream of mushroom soup

1/2 cup mayonnaise

1/2 cup milk

Stir all ingredients together in a large bowl.

Grease a 2 1/2-quart baking dish and pour in ingredients.

Bake at 375° F for 25 minutes.

Serves 6

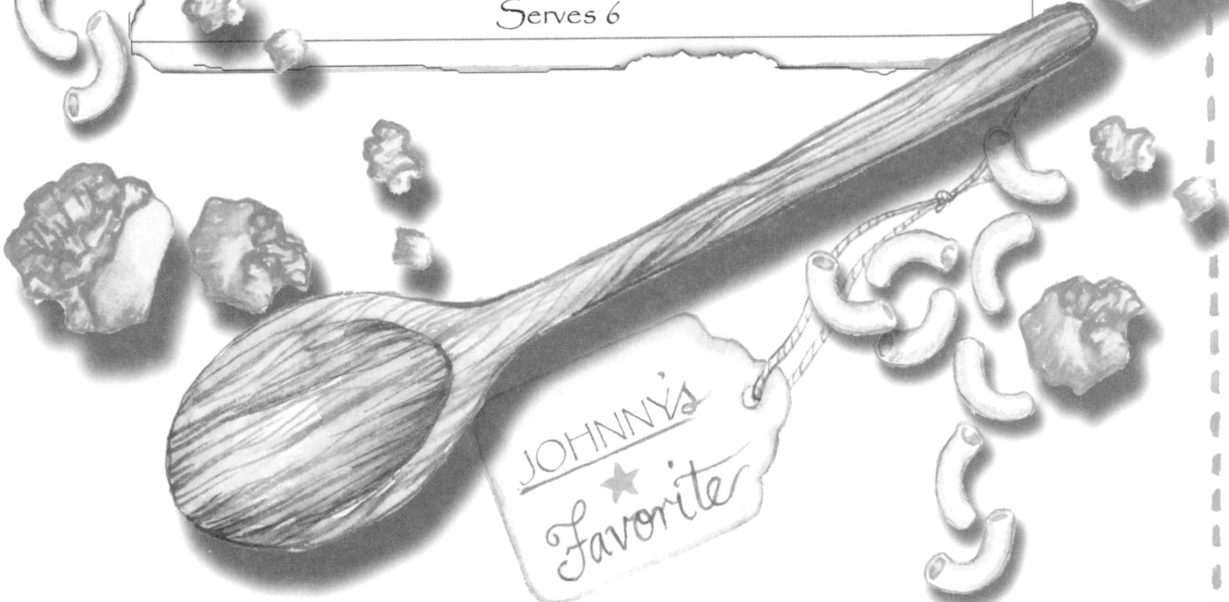

JOHNNY'S ★ Favorite

NOTE: You may substitute low-fat cheese, fat-free soup, fat-free milk and low-fat mayonnaise, if you desire.

SMOKED SALMON SPAGHETTI

1 lb. spaghetti
2 tbsp olive oil
1 1/4 cups half-and-half
2/3 cup whiskey or brandy
4 1/2 oz. smoked salmon
Black pepper
2 tbsp chopped fresh parsley
1/2 cup crumbled feta cheese

Cook spaghetti in salted water with one tbsp of the olive oil until tender but firm.
Drain and return to the pot; sprinkle with remaining olive oil and stir slightly to coat.
Pour the half-and-half into a small saucepan and bring to simmering, but do not boil.
In another small pan, pour whiskey and bring to simmer, but do not boil.
Remove both pans from the heat and mix together the half-and-half and the whiskey.
Cut the smoked salmon into thin strips and add to the half-and-half mixture. Season with black pepper.
Just before serving, mix in fresh parsley. Transfer spaghetti to a serving dish and pour sauce over and toss thoroughly.
Sprinkle crumbled feta cheese on top.

Serves 4

STRAW and HAY

4 tbsp butter or margarine
14-oz. pkg. frozen peas
1 cup half-and-half
1 lb. green and white linguine pasta
1 tbsp olive oil
1 cup grated Parmesan cheese, freshly grated if possible
1/4 tsp grated nutmeg
Salt and pepper to taste

Melt butter or margarine in a large pan. Add the peas and cook on low 2 minutes, or until just tender.
Pour 2/3 cup of half-and-half into the pan, bring to boil and simmer for 1 to 2 minutes, or until the mixture is slightly thickened. Remove from heat. In the meantime, cook pasta in salted water with olive oil until tender but firm. Drain, and return to the pot.
Add the peas and cream to the pasta; heat on medium. Add the remaining half-and-half and the grated Parmesan cheese. Add the nutmeg and season to taste with salt and pepper. Heat through, tossing gently.
Transfer to serving dish and serve immediately, sprinkled with extra Parmesan cheese.

Makes 4 servings

I love bread. From biscuits to muffins to plain old white bread slathered with butter, they are all s-o-o very good. My mother is a whiz at making breads from just about anything—vegetables, fruits, cheese, etc. Here, I have tried to provide a variety of recipes to appeal to all kinds of tastes. I particularly love the Ever-ready Bran Muffins, which are not only delicious but very handy as you can prepare the batter ahead of time and use it as needed. And biscuits at our house were practically a daily staple. Growing up, I also remember cornbread as being my father's favorite. Crumbled in a bowl with buttermilk poured over it, it was his nightly ritual. Personally, that is not my favorite way of eating it, but to each his own.

Quick Breads, Biscuits and Muffins

CARROT BREAD

1 1/2 cups all-purpose flour
1 1/2 tsp baking soda
1 1/2 tsp cinnamon
1/2 tsp salt
1 cup pecans (optional)
2 eggs
3/4 cup sugar
1 cup salad oil
1 tsp vanilla extract
1 1/2 cups carrot pieces

Heat oven to 350° F. Grease a 9x5x3-inch loaf pan. Assemble blender.

Sift flour, baking soda, cinnamon and salt into a large mixing bowl; set aside.

Blender chop nuts. Add to dry ingredients.

Put eggs, sugar, oil and vanilla extract into blender container; cover and process at mix until smooth. Stop blender, and add carrot pieces; cover and process four times at liquefy. Pour over ingredients and mix only until dry ingredients are moistened.

Pour into prepared pan and bake 1 hour or until cake tester comes out clean. Cool 5 minutes in pan, then turn out onto cake rack to cool.

Makes 1 loaf

ZUCCHINI NUT BREAD

Shortening
Flour
3 cups flour
1 tsp baking powder
1 tsp baking soda
1 tsp cinnamon
1 tsp nutmeg
1 cup chopped pecans
1/4 cup vegetable oil
3 eggs
2 cups sugar
2 tsp vanilla
3 cups unpeeled, shredded zucchini squash

Preheat oven to 350° F. Grease and flour 2 loaf pans with shortening and flour.
In a large bowl, mix 3 cups flour, baking powder, soda, cinnamon, nutmeg and pecans. Stir until blended.
Make a well in the center of the mixture.
In a medium bowl, combine oil, eggs, sugar and vanilla; mix well.
Stir in shredded zucchini. Pour mixture into well of dry ingredients and stir until moistened. Spoon mixture into the two prepared pans.
Bake for 1 hour or until a knife inserted in center of loaf comes out clean.
Cool in pans for 10 minutes; then remove to cooling rack.

Makes 2 loaves

CORNBREAD

2 heaping tbsp shortening
2 cups cornmeal mix
Approx. 2 tbsp self-rising flour
1 cup plus buttermilk

Preheat oven to 400º F. Put the shortening in an iron skillet and place in oven to melt. Stir cornmeal and flour together.
Add buttermilk until you have a thin batter. Add hot shortening to batter; stir well.
Pour mixture into skillet (leave a little melted shortening in the pan).
Bake 25 to 30 minutes or until golden brown.

Makes about 12 servings

NOTE: I use low-fat buttermilk. I don't know how much difference it makes in calories, but the guilt factor goes way down. Also, it is a great idea to save any leftover cornbread in a Ziploc bag in the freezer. You can use it later to make cornbread dressing with chicken.

A Southern favorite!

CRANBERRY BREAD

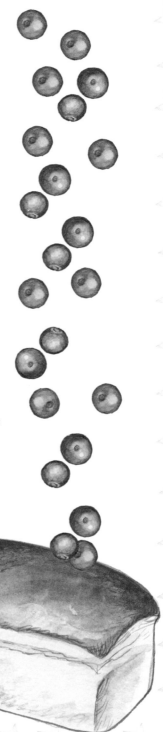

4 cups all-purpose flour
2 cups sugar
1 tbsp baking powder
2 tsp salt
1/2 cup shortening
2 eggs
1 3/4 cups orange juice
2 tbsp grated orange peel
2 cups fresh or frozen cranberries, chopped
1 cup chopped walnuts

In a large mixing bowl, mix first four ingredients. Cut in shortening with a pastry blender until mixture resembles coarse crumbs.
In a medium bowl, beat with a fork eggs, orange juice and grated orange peel; stir into flour mixture until flour is moistened.
Gently stir cranberries and walnuts into batter.
Spoon batter into two greased and floured 9x5-inch loaf pans.
Bake at 350º F for 55 minutes or until toothpick inserted in center comes out clean. Let cool in pan for 10 minutes then remove to cooling rack.

Makes 2 loaves

NOTE: Makes a great snack or appetizer served with cream cheese.

MONKEY BREAD
(SWEET)

4 cans biscuits (any type)
1 tbsp cinnamon
1/2 cup nuts (ground finely)
3/4 cup sugar
2 sticks margarine or butter (melted)

Cut each biscuit into 4 pieces.
Preheat oven to 350º F.
Spray a round tube pan with cooking spray.
Mix cinnamon, nuts and sugar in a small bowl.
Roll each piece of biscuit in melted butter, then in
nut mixture.
Place each piece around the perimeter of pan evenly.
Bake for approx. 40 minutes or until golden brown.
Let stand in pan for 5 to 10 minutes before turning out
onto dish.

Approx. 8 servings

NOTE: This monkey bread is great for
brunch or breakfast with a hot cup of coffee.

MONKEY BREAD (SPICY)

4 cans biscuits (any type)
1 cup grated Parmesan cheese
1/2 cup finely chopped onions
1/2 cup chopped red bell peppers
2 sticks margarine or butter (melted)

Cut each biscuit into 4 pieces.
Preheat oven to 350° F.
Spray a round tube pan with cooking spray.
Mix cheese, onions and peppers in a small bowl.
Roll each piece of biscuit in melted butter or margarine then in cheese mixture.
Place each piece around the perimeter of pan evenly.
Bake for approx. 40 minutes or until golden brown.
Let stand in pan for 5 to 10 minutes before turning out onto dish.

Approx. 8 servings

NOTE: This monkey bread is great served with an Italian pasta dish and salad.

CHEDDAR DILL BREAD

2 cups self-rising flour
1 tbsp sugar
1/2 stick butter or margarine
1 cup shredded sharp Cheddar cheese
2 tsp dill weed
1 egg
3/4 cup milk

In a large bowl, combine flour and sugar. Cut in butter until crumbly; stir in cheese and dill. In a small bowl, beat egg and milk; pour into dry ingredients and stir just until moistened. (Batter will be very thick.) Pour into greased 8x4x2-inch loaf pan. Bake at 350º F for 35 to 40 minutes or until bread tests done. Cool in pan for 10 minutes before removing to a wire rack.

Makes 1 loaf

NOTE: This is a great bread to serve with soup or chili.

LEMONADE BREAD

1 tbsp frozen lemonade concentrate
1/2 cup shortening
1 cup sugar
1 1/2 cups plain flour
2 tsp baking powder
1/2 cup milk
2 eggs
1/3 cup frozen lemonade concentrate

Preheat over to 350º F. Combine all
ingredients except the 1/3 cup lemonade.
Blend well and beat 3 minutes at medium
speed on mixer.
Pour batter into greased 9x5-inch pan.
Bake for 50 to 60 minutes.
Loosen bread from edges of pan. When
done, spread 1/3 cup lemonade concentrate
over bread. Cool, remove from pan and serve.

Makes 1 loaf

NOTE: This is great served
with a fruit salad or sorbet.

ENGLISH MUFFIN BREAD

2 cups milk
1/2 cup water
2 tbsp cornmeal
6 cups bread flour
2 pkg. active dry yeast
1 tbsp sugar
2 tsp salt
1/4 tsp baking soda

Warm the milk and water in a small saucepan until very warm.
Lightly grease two 8x4-inch loaf pans; sprinkle cornmeal inside the pans.
In a large bowl, mix together 3 cups flour, the yeast, sugar, salt and baking soda.
Stir milk into the flour mixture; beat well.
Stir in the remaining flour, 1 cup at a time until it forms a stiff batter.
Spoon the batter into the greased cornmeal coated pans.
Cover and place in a warm place to rise for about 45 minutes or until doubled in size.
In the meantime, preheat the oven to 400º F.
Bake in preheated oven until golden brown, about 25 minutes.
Remove from pans; cool.

Makes 2 loaves

HUSH PUPPIES

2 1/4 cups self-rising white cornmeal mix
2 tbsp self-rising flour
1/2 medium onion, chopped
1 tsp salt
1/2 tsp ground black pepper
1 cup buttermilk
2 large eggs
Vegetable oil

Combine first 5 ingredients in a large mixing bowl. Make a well in the center of the mixture.
Whisk buttermilk and eggs together in a small bowl. Add to dry ingredients; stir until moistened. Let stand for about 15 minutes.
Pour oil about 2-inches deep in electric skillet. Heat to 375° F.
Drop batter by heaping tablespoonfuls into the hot oil. Cook 2 minutes on each side or until golden brown. Drain on paper towels.

6 to 8 servings

BISCUITS

2 cups self-rising flour
1/3 cup shortening
3/4 cup buttermilk

Heat oven to 350° F. Cut shortening into flour by hand. Pour in buttermilk all at once. Mix into a soft dough. Turn out onto floured board, pat or roll out to 1/2-inch thickness and cut with a floured biscuit cutter. Place in greased pan. Bake for 12 to 15 minutes or until golden brown.

Makes approx. 12 biscuits

NOTE: I don't roll my biscuits out and cut them. I roll them in my hand till the shape is that of a flattened ball. I also brush the tops with a bit of buttermilk.

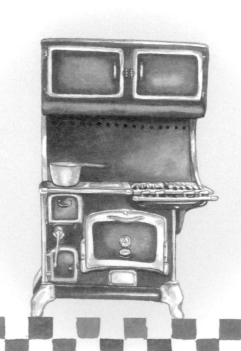

ANGEL BISCUITS

1 pkg. active dry yeast
4 to 4 1/2 cups self-rising flour
1 tsp sugar
2/3 cup shortening
1/2 cup warm water
1 cup milk or 1 1/4 cups buttermilk

Grease three 8-inch round cake pans. Dissolve yeast in warm water; set aside. Stir flour and sugar together. Cut in shortening until "pea" size. Stir in yeast, water and milk until dough begins to pull away from bowl. Turn out onto floured surface and knead gently ten to twelve times. Roll 1/2-inch thick, and cut with a 2-inch cutter. Place 8 to 10 biscuits in each prepared pan. Cover with wax paper. Put in a warm place to rise for 1 hour. Heat oven to 400° F. Bake 20 to 25 minutes or until golden brown.

Makes 2 to 2 1/2 dozen biscuits

QUICK EASY MUFFINS

2 cups self-rising flour
2 heaping tbsp mayonnaise
1 cup milk
Grated cheese (optional)

Blend all ingredients in a medium-size mixing
bowl.
Drop by spoonfuls into a greased muffin pan.
Bake at 450° F for about 20 minutes.
One cup grated cheese may be added to mixture
for cheese muffins.

Makes 12 muffins

EVER-READY BRAN MUFFINS

15-oz. box wheat bran flakes cereal with raisins
1 tbsp plus 2 tsp baking soda
2 tsp salt
5 cups all-purpose flour
3 cups sugar
4 eggs, beaten
1 quart buttermilk
1 cup vegetable oil

Combine first five ingredients in a very large bowl. Make a well in the center of mixture. Add eggs, buttermilk and oil; stir just enough to moisten dry ingredients. Cover and store in refrigerator until ready to bake. Batter will keep up to 6 weeks. To bake, spoon batter into greased muffin pan, filling 2/3 full. Bake at 400º F for 12 to 15 minutes.

Makes about 5 dozen muffins

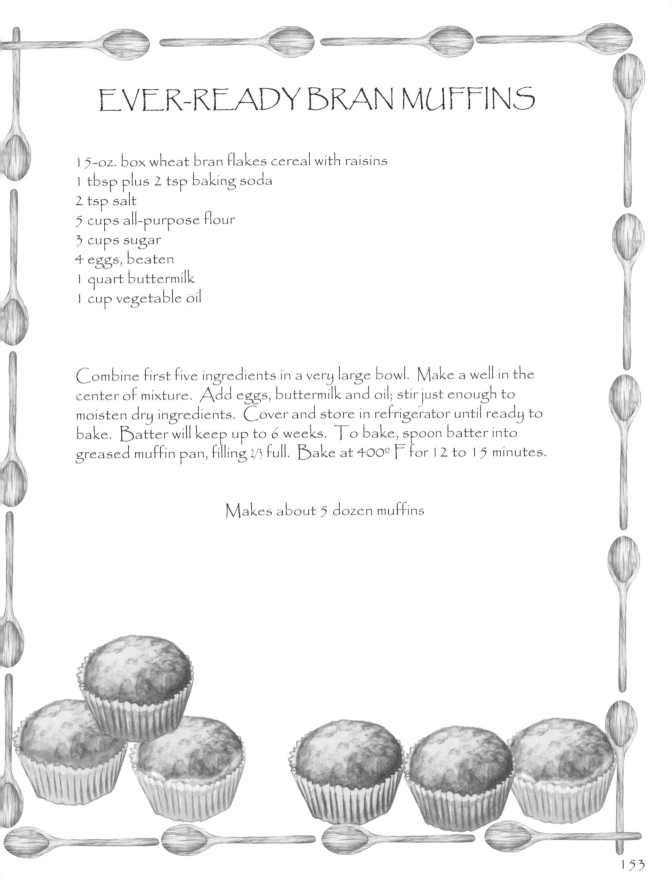

RASPBERRY SOUR CREAM MUFFINS

TOPPING
2 tbsp chopped pecans
2 tbsp sugar
1 tbsp wheat germ

MUFFINS
1 1/4 cups all-purpose flour
1/2 cup wheat germ
1/2 cup sugar
2 tsp baking powder
1 tsp ground cinnamon

1/4 tsp salt
1/2 cup sour cream
1/2 cup skim milk
1 egg, beaten
1 cup fresh raspberries, rinsed
and patted dry

GLAZE
1/2 cup powdered sugar
1 tbsp fresh lemon juice

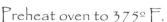

Preheat oven to 375° F.
For topping: Combine all ingredients in a small bowl; set aside.
For muffins: Combine flour, wheat germ, sugar, baking powder,
cinnamon and salt in a large bowl. Mix well.
In a medium bowl, combine sour cream, milk and egg; blend well.
Add all at once to dry ingredients; mix just until dry ingredients
are moistened. Gently fold in raspberries.
Fill paper-lined muffin cups almost full.
Sprinkle with topping.
Bake 25 minutes or until toothpick inserted in center comes
out clean. Cool muffins in pan for 5 minutes; remove from pan.
For glaze: Combine powdered
sugar and lemon juice in a small bowl; mix
until smooth. Drizzle over muffins. Serve
warm.

Makes 1 dozen muffins

MOCHA CHOCOLATE CHIP BANANA MUFFINS

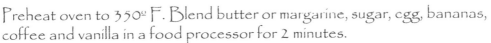

1 cup butter or margarine
1 1/4 cups sugar
1 egg
3 ripe bananas
1 tbsp instant coffee, dissolved in 1 tbsp water
1 tsp vanilla
2 1/4 cups all-purpose flour
1/4 tsp salt
1 tsp baking powder
1 tsp baking soda
1 cup semi-sweet chocolate chips

Preheat oven to 350º F. Blend butter or margarine, sugar, egg, bananas, coffee and vanilla in a food processor for 2 minutes.
Add flour, salt, baking powder and baking soda. Blend until flour disappears.
Add chocolate chips and mix in with a wooden spoon.
Spoon mixture into paper-lined muffin cups.
Bake for 25 minutes. Cool on a wire rack.

Makes 12 to 18 muffins

Pineapple Upside-down Cake is one of my all-time childhood favorites. My father's sister Polly made the best I ever tasted. She has been gone for many years now, but I think of her every time I have it. When I was growing up, cakes were often reserved just for holidays; so memories of family get-togethers are part of the pleasure of eating these. My personal choice for my birthday cake was the German Chocolate Cake. The Punch Bowl Cake is moist and delicious and the recipe for Autumn Pudding is my own invention that my children love. But the absolute family favorite, hands down, is Chocolate Delight. Enjoy.

Desserts

PINEAPPLE UPSIDE-DOWN CAKE

1/4 cup margarine
1 cup packed brown sugar
20-oz. can sliced pineapple, drained,
 reserve liquid
6-oz. jar maraschino cherries, drained
1 pkg. yellow cake mix

Preheat over to 350º F. Melt margarine in
a 13x9x2-inch pan.
Sprinkle brown sugar over margarine.
Arrange pineapple slices and cherries
over brown sugar, press gently.
Prepare cake mix according to package
directions, except use pineapple juice in
place of some of the liquid required.
Pour over pineapple and cherries.
Bake for 40 to 45 minutes or until
toothpick inserted in center comes out
clean.
Remove from oven and turn upside down
on a serving platter. Leave pan over cake
for 1-2 minutes before removing.

Makes 10 to 12 servings

My Aunt Polly made this famous...at least
in my fanily.

FRESH APPLE POUND CAKE

1 1/4 cups vegetable oil
2 cups sugar
3 eggs
3 cups sifted flour
1 tsp salt
1 tsp baking soda
2 tsp vanilla
3 large apples, chopped
1 cup chopped pecans

In a large mixing bowl, combine oil, sugar and eggs; beat at medium speed for 3 minutes. In a medium bowl, combine flour, salt and soda. Add to oil and sugar mixture. Add vanilla. Fold in apples and pecans. Pour into a greased and floured tube cake pan. Bake at 325º F for 1 hour and 20 minutes. Cool. Glaze with brown sugar glaze below.

GLAZE
3 tbsp butter
3 tbsp light brown sugar
3 tbsp cream or condensed milk
3 tbsp sugar
1/4 tsp vanilla
Combine all ingredients in a medium saucepan until mixture thickens. Pour over warm cake on serving dish.

Serves 10 to 12

FRUIT COCKTAIL CAKE

3 eggs
2 1/2 cups sugar
2 1/2 cups self-rising flour
8-oz. can fruit cocktail
1 tsp vanilla

In a large bowl, beat eggs, then add all other ingredients; mix and pour into three greased and floured 9-inch cake pans.
Bake at 350° F for 30 minutes, or until cake leaves sides of pan.
Remove from pans and cool.

ICING
2 sticks margarine
1 1/2 cups sugar
2/3 cup milk
1 cup chopped pecans
1 cup coconut
1 tsp vanilla

Combine all ingredients in a small saucepan and cook over medium heat for 2 to 3 minutes.
Spread over cake layers while still hot.

Serves 10 to 12

POPPY SEED CAKE

3 cups flour
2 1/3 cups sugar
1 1/2 tsp salt
1 1/2 tsp baking powder
3 eggs
1 1/2 cups milk
1 1/8 cups oil
3 tsp poppy seeds
1 1/2 tsp vanilla
1 1/2 tsp almond flavoring
1 1/2 tsp butter flavoring

GLAZE
1/4 cup orange juice
3/4 cup sugar
1/2 tsp vanilla
1/2 tsp almond flavoring

In a large mixing bowl, combine all ingredients and mix well.   Pour into 2 greased and floured loaf pans.   Bake at 325º F for 1 hour.

In a medium bowl, mix glaze ingredients together until blended. Pour over cake while it is cooling in the pan.

Serves 10 to 12

POUND CAKE

1 cup shortening
1 stick margarine
2 3/4 cups sugar
1 cup milk
3 cups all-purpose flour
1/2 tsp salt
1/2 tsp baking powder
1 tsp vanilla
5 eggs

Place all ingredients in a large mixing bowl; beat until very smooth. Pour into a greased and floured tube pan and bake in 325º F oven for 1 hour and 15 minutes.

Serves 8 to 10

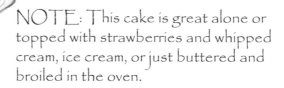

NOTE: This cake is great alone or topped with strawberries and whipped cream, ice cream, or just buttered and broiled in the oven.

RED VELVET CAKE

1/2 cup shortening
1 1/2 cups sugar
2 eggs
2 oz. red cake coloring or 1 small bottle
1 tbsp cocoa
2 1/2 cups plain flour
1 tsp salt
1 cup buttermilk
1 tsp baking soda
1 tbsp vinegar

In a large mixing bowl, cream shortening with an electric mixer; add sugar.
Add eggs, one at a time, beating after each addition.
Add cake coloring and cocoa.
In a medium bowl, sift flour and salt together; add to shortening and sugar
mixture, alternating with buttermilk. Fold in soda and vinegar.
Pour into 3 greased and floured 9-inch cake pans.
Bake at 350º F for 30 to 35 minutes.
Cool layers and frost.

Serves 10 to 12

Frost with
CREAM CHEESE FROSTING
See Hummingbird Cake for recipe.

GERMAN CHOCOLATE CAKE

4-oz. pkg. German sweet chocolate
1/2 cup boiling water
2 ½ cups all-purpose flour
1/2 tsp salt
1 tsp baking soda
1 cup butter or margarine
2 cups sugar
4 eggs, separated
1 tsp vanilla
1 cup buttermilk

Melt chocolate in a double-boiler pan; set aside to cool.
Sift together flour, salt and soda into a medium bowl; set aside.
In a large bowl, use an electric mixer to cream butter with sugar until fluffy.
Add egg yolks one at a time, beat well after each addition.
Add melted chocolate and vanilla.
Add dry ingredients alternately with buttermilk. Beat until smooth.
In a separate bowl, whip egg whites until they form peaks, then fold into batter with a spoon.
Pour into three greased and floured 9-inch round cake pans.
Bake at 350º F for 35 to 40 minutes.
Remove from pan and cool on a rack.

FROSTING

1 cup evaporated milk
1 cup sugar
3 egg yolks
1 stick margarine or butter
1 1/3 cups coconut
1 cup chopped pecans
1 tsp vanilla

Combine all ingredients and cook over medium heat until the mixture thickens. Stir and cool until thick enough to spread on top and between chocolate cake layers. Frost between, on top and on sides of layers.

Serves 10 to 12

COFFEE CAKE

3 cups flour
1 1/2 cups sugar
3 eggs
1/4 cup orange juice
3/4 cup vegetable oil
3 tsp baking powder
1 can pie filling, any flavor
3 tbsp cinnamon
3 tbsp sugar

Mix first six ingredients together in a large mixing bowl.
Pour half of batter into a greased and floured 13x9x2-inch pan.
Spread pie filling over batter and cover with the rest of the cake batter.
In a small bowl mix cinnamon and sugar; sprinkle over top.
Bake at 350º F for 45 to 55 minutes or until toothpick inserted in the center comes out clean.

Serves 8

APPLE CHEESECAKE

1 cup graham cracker crumbs
1/2 cup finely chopped pecans
3 tbsp white sugar
1/2 tsp ground cinnamon
1/4 cup unsalted butter, melted
2 8-oz. pkg. cream cheese,
 softened
1/2 cup white sugar

2 eggs
1/2 tsp vanilla
1/3 cup white sugar
1/2 teaspoon ground cinnamon
4 cups apples, peeled, cored, and
 sliced thin
1/4 cup chopped pecans

Preheat oven to 350º F. In a large bowl, stir together the graham cracker
crumbs, 1/2 cup pecans, 3 tbsp sugar, 1/2 tsp cinnamon and the melted butter;
press into the bottom of a 9-inch springform pan. Bake in preheated oven for
10 minutes.
In a large bowl, combine cream cheese and 1/2 cup sugar. Mix at medium speed
until smooth. Beat in eggs one at a time. Mix well after each addition.
Blend in vanilla; pour filling into the baked crust.
In a small bowl, stir together 1/3 cup sugar and 1/2 tsp cinnamon. Toss the
cinnamon sugar with the apples to coat. Spoon apple mixture over the cream
cheese layer and sprinkle with 1/4 cup chopped pecans. Bake in preheated
over for 1 hour to 1 hour 10 minutes. With a knife, loosen the cake from
the rim of the pan. Let cool, and then remove the rim of the pan. Chill before
serving.

Makes 12 servings

PUNCH BOWL CAKE

1 box yellow cake mix
2 large boxes vanilla instant pudding mix
2 large cans crushed pineapple, drained
1 can (21-oz.) cherry pie filling
1 large container whipped topping
1 cup chopped nuts, lightly toasted

Prepare cake (make 2 layers) and pudding according to package directions.
Crumble one layer of prepared cake into the bottom of a glass punch bowl. Pour half the pudding over cake.
Crumble other layer of cake into the punch bowl and pour rest of pudding mix over that.
Add pineapple, then cherry pie filling, followed by whipped topping.
Sprinkle nuts on top and refrigerate for several hours before serving.

Makes 10 to 12 servings

CHOCOLATE POUND CAKE

3 cups flour
4 heaping tbsp cocoa
1/2 tsp salt
1/2 tsp baking powder
1 1/2 cups shortening
3 cups sugar
5 eggs
1 1/4 cups milk
2 tsp vanilla

Sift flour, cocoa, salt and baking powder three times into a medium bowl.
In a large mixing bowl, cream shortening and sugar until creamy. Add eggs; beat well. Add milk and flour mixture, alternating; beat well. Add vanilla. Pour into a greased and floured tube cake pan. Bake at 325° F for 1 1/2 hours. Cool.
Frost with Creamy Chocolate Glaze, if desired.

CREAMY CHOCOLATE GLAZE

2 1/4 cups powdered sugar
3 tbsp cocoa
1/4 cup margarine, softened
3 to 4 tbsp milk

Combine sugar and cocoa in a medium bowl; mix well. Add remaining ingredients. Using an electric mixer, beat until smooth. Spread on cake.   Serves 10 to 12

YUMMY CHOCOLATE SHEET CAKE

2 cups sugar
2 cups sifted flour
1 tsp baking soda
1 tsp salt
1 cup butter or margarine
1 cup water
1/4 cup cocoa
1/2 cup buttermilk
2 eggs, beaten
1 tsp vanilla

ICING
1 stick margarine
3 tbsp cocoa
6 tbsp milk
1 box powdered sugar
1 tsp vanilla
3 cups chopped nuts

For cake: Sift sugar, flour, soda and salt into
a medium bowl. In a large saucepan, melt
butter, add water and cocoa; stir constantly.
Bring to a rolling boil over medium heat.
Add dry ingredients; mix well.
Stir in buttermilk, eggs and vanilla.
Pour into a 15x10x1-inch greased and
floured pan. Bake in 400° F oven for
20 to 25 minutes.

For icing: Bring margarine, cocoa
and milk to boiling in a small saucepan.
Add powdered sugar, vanilla and
nuts until blended. Cool slightly.
Frost cake while still warm.

Serve 10 to 12

HUMMINGBIRD CAKE

3 cups all-purpose flour
2 cups sugar
1 tsp baking soda
1 tsp salt
1 tsp cinnamon
3 eggs, beaten
1 cup vegetable oil
1 1/2 tsp vanilla
8-oz. can crushed
 pineapple, undrained
2 cups chopped bananas
1 cup chopped pecans

CREAM CHEESE FROSTING
8-oz. pkg. cream cheese
1 stick margarine
16-oz. pkg. powdered sugar
1 tsp vanilla
1/2 cup chopped pecans

Combine first five ingredients in a large mixing bowl; add eggs and oil, stirring until dry ingredients are moistened. Do not beat.
Stir in vanilla, pineapple, bananas and 1 cup pecans. Spoon into three greased and floured 9-inch cake pans.
Bake at 350° F for 25 to 30 minutes, or until a toothpick inserted in center comes out clean. Cool for 10 minutes in pans.
Remove from pans and cool completely.

To make frosting: combine cream cheese and margarine; beat with electric mixer until smooth. Add powdered sugar and vanilla; beat until light and fluffy. Spread frosting between layers and on top and sides. Sprinkle with 1/2 cup chopped pecans.

Serves 10 to 12

JAPANESE FRUIT CAKE

1 cup butter or margarine
2 cups sugar
4 eggs
3 cups all-purpose flour
1/2 tsp salt
1 tsp baking soda
1 tsp cinnamon
1 tsp allspice
1 tsp ground cloves
1 tsp nutmeg
1 cup buttermilk
1 cup chopped nuts
1 cup chopped raisins
2 to 3 tbsp flour

Cream butter and sugar together.
Add eggs, one at a time; beat well after each addition. Sift dry ingredients together.
Add the two mixtures together, alternating with buttermilk.
Flour nuts and raisins in a small bowl with the 2 or 3 tbsp flour. Add to batter.
Divide batter between three 9-inch greased and floured cake pans.
Bake at 300º F for one hour, or until cake releases slightly from side of pan.

Assemble with COCONUT LEMON GLAZE between layers and on top.

COCONUT LEMON GLAZE

2 7-oz. cans or pkg. coconut
2 1/2 cups sugar
2 tbsp flour
1 1/2 cups hot water
2 lemons, juice and grated rind

Combine all ingredients in a medium saucepan.
Cook until thickened over medium heat, stirring
often.
Cool slightly before putting on the fruit cake.
Divide between top and between layers.

Serves 10 to 12

BASIC PIE CRUST

1 cup all-purpose flour
1/2 tsp salt
1/3 cup shortening
3 tbsp cold water

In a medium mixing bowl, sift the flour and salt together.
Add the shortening, cut in with a pastry blender until it looks like coarse crumbs.
Sprinkle with cold water, one tbsp at a time.
Mix lightly until the mixture sticks together and bowl is 'clean'.
Roll out the dough on a floured board to 1/8-inch thick, and 1 inch larger than your pie pan.
Pat and fit the dough into your pan without stretching or pulling.
Cut off edges leaving 1/2-inch to 1-inch overhang for a single crust.
Crimp edges between your thumb and forefinger along edge of pan.
With a fork, pierce a few holes in the bottom and sides of the dough.
Bake in a preheated 450° F oven for 10 to 15 minutes or until golden brown.

Makes 1 crust

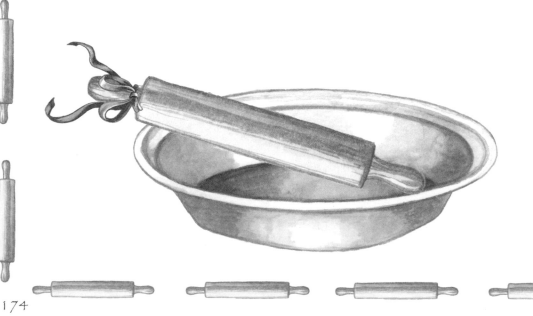

RAISIN PIE

2 cups water
2 cups raisins
1/2 cup sugar
3 tbsp flour
1/4 cup lemon juice
1/2 cup chopped nuts
Unbaked pie shell for 2-crust pie

Bring water to boiling in a medium saucepan. Add raisins. Cover and cook for 5 minutes.
Mix sugar and flour in a large mixing bowl, stir into saucepan with raisins.
Cook, stirring constantly until boiling. Boil for 1 minute. Remove from heat.
Stir in lemon juice; add nuts. Pour into unbaked piecrust.
Cover with top crust.
Bake at 425° F for 30 minutes or until golden brown.

Makes 8 servings

PECAN PIE

3 eggs, slightly beaten
1 cup Karo corn syrup
1 cup sugar
2 tbsp butter or margarine, melted
1 tsp vanilla
1 1/2 cups chopped pecans
1 unbaked pie crust shell, 8 or 9-inch

In a large bowl, mix eggs, syrup, sugar, butter and
vanilla until well blended. Stir in nuts. Pour into pastry
shell.
Bake at 350° F for 50 to 55 minutes, or until knife
inserted halfway between center and edge comes out
clean. Cool and serve.

Makes 8 servings

FRIED APPLE PIES

2 apples
1/3 cup sugar
1/2 tsp ground cinnamon
2 cups all-purpose flour
1 tsp salt
1/2 cup shortening
1/2 cup cold water
1 cup vegetable oil
Powdered sugar (optional)

Peel and dice apples. Add sugar and cinnamon.
Cook in a saucepan on low heat. Cook until soft, then mash
with a fork to form a thick applesauce.

Sift flour and salt together. Cut in the
shortening. Add water and mix with a fork.
Roll out on a floured board to 1/8-inch thick.
Cut with a large cookie cutter into 4-inch
circles. In each circle, place 1 heaping tbsp
fruit. Moisten edges with water, fold over and
press edges together with a fork.
Heat oil in a large skillet on medium-high heat.
Fry pies a couple at a time until golden
brown, about 2 to 3 minutes on each side.

Drain on paper
towels. Sprinkle with
powdered sugar, if desired.

Makes 6 to 8 pies

NOTHING PIE

1 cup sugar
3 eggs
3 tsp flour

1 1/2 tsp vanilla
1/4 cup margarine
8-oz. can evaporated milk

In a large bowl, mix all ingredients. Pour into a greased 9-inch pie pan.
Bake at 350º F until set and golden brown on top, about 30 minutes.

Serves 8

BUTTERMILK PIE

1 1/4 cups sugar
1 tbsp flour
2 eggs
3/4 stick butter or margarine, melted
1 cup buttermilk
2 tsp vanilla
8 or 9-inch unbaked pie shell

In a large bowl, mix sugar and flour. Add eggs, butter, buttermilk
and vanilla. Pour into pie shell and bake at 450º F for 10 minutes.
Turn oven heat down to 350º F and bake for 30 minutes more.

Serves 8

LEMON MERINGUE PIE

FILLING
1 1/3 cups sweetened condensed milk
1/2 cup RealLemon reconstituted lemon juice
2 egg yolks
8 or 9-inch crumb or baked pastry pie shell

In a medium mixing bowl, blend milk, lemon juice, and egg yolks until thickened.
Pour into pie shell.

MERINGUE
2 egg whites, at room temperature
1/4 tsp cream of tartar
1/4 cup sugar

In a small mixing bowl, whip whites and cream of tartar until they hold a stiff peak.
Gradually whip in sugar only until whites hold firm peaks.
Pile onto pie filling and seal to inside edge of pie shell.
Bake at 325º F until golden brown, about 15 minutes. Cool.
Chill pie.

Serves 8

BREAD PUDDING

4 to 5 cold biscuits
1 1/2 cups boiling water
1 stick margarine
1 tsp vanilla
2 beaten eggs
1 cup sugar
8-oz. can evaporated milk

Crumble biscuits into a large mixing bowl.
Cover with boiling water; let cool slightly.
Add margarine; stir to melt. Add remaining ingredients.
Pour into a greased 2-quart baking dish.
Bake at 350° F for 30 minutes. Check midway
through cooking time. When pudding begins to
set around the edges of pan, stir away from
sides and continue to cook until set.

VARIATION: For chocolate
pudding, add 2 tbsp cocoa to mixture
before cooking.

Serves 8 to 10

AUTUMN PUDDING

1 large box instant vanilla pudding
1 cup half-and-half
15 1/2-oz. can pumpkin pie mix
15 to 20 full-size cinnamon-covered graham crackers
1 bag Heath bar pieces
Large marshmallows

In a large bowl, using an electric mixer, blend pudding mix and half-and-half
until slightly thickened. Add pumpkin pie mix; mix well.
In a 12x12-inch pan, place crackers in a single layer.
Pour approximately one third of the pudding mixture over.
Sprinkle with 1/3 of the Heath pieces, repeat layers 2 more times.
Cut marshmallows in half and place cut-side down on top of last layer.
Place in oven on broil just long enough to lightly brown the marshmallows.
Cool slightly and serve.

Makes 10 to 12 servings

BANANA PUDDING

1 cup sugar
2 tbsp flour
2 eggs
2 cups milk
1 tsp vanilla
1 tbsp butter or margarine
1 box vanilla wafers
3 or 4 large bananas

Mix sugar, flour, eggs and milk in a medium saucepan.
Cook over medium heat until thickened. Remove from heat; add vanilla and butter.
In a medium serving bowl or trifle bowl, place one layer of vanilla wafers in bottom.
Slice bananas over wafers, followed by pudding, continue layering until all ingredients are gone. End with wafers on top.

Serves 8 to 10

NOTE: In place of bananas, you can substitute: strawberries, coconut or pineapple. If you wish, you may top with meringue (see Lemon Meringue Pie for directions) or with whipped topping.

FUDGE PUDDING

2 tbsp melted margarine
1 cup sugar
1 tsp vanilla
1 cup sifted flour
8 tbsp cocoa
1 tsp baking powder
1/2 tsp salt
1/2 cup milk
1 2/3 cups boiling water

In a medium bowl, mix margarine, 1/2 cup sugar and vanilla together.
Into another medium bowl, sift flour, 3 tbsp cocoa, baking powder and
1/4 tsp salt.
Add this to margarine and sugar mixture alternating with milk. Mix well.
In a 10x6x2-inch baking dish, mix remaining 1/2 cup sugar, remaining 5
tbsp of cocoa, the remaining 1/4 tsp salt and boiling water.
Drop the batter into the liquid in the baking dish by heaping
tablespoonfuls.
Bake at 350º F for 40 to 45 minutes. Serve warm.

Makes 8 to 10 servings

RICE PUDDING

1 1/2 cups cooked white rice
2 cups milk, divided
1/3 cup white sugar
1/4 tsp salt
1 egg, beaten
2/3 cup golden raisins
1 tbsp butter
1/2 tsp vanilla

In a medium saucepan, combine cooked rice, 1 1/2 cups milk, sugar and salt. Cook over medium heat until thick and creamy, about 15 to 20 minutes.

Stir in remaining milk, beaten egg and raisins. Cook 2 minutes more, stirring constantly.

Remove from heat and stir in butter and vanilla. Serve warm.

Serves 4

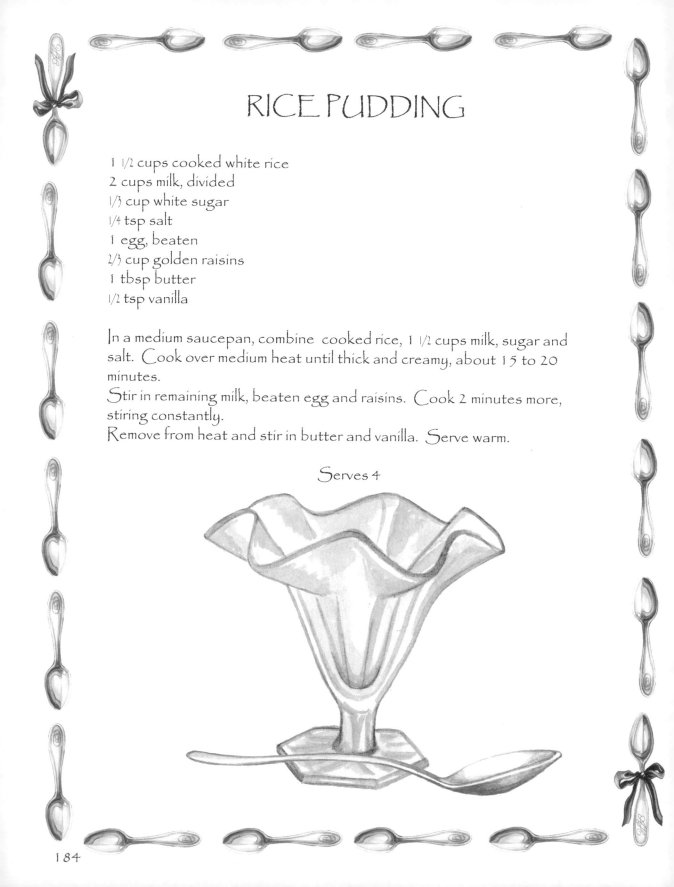

SWEET POTATO COBBLER

3 or 4 sweet potatoes
1/4 cup sugar
Water
1/2 cup butter or margarine
1 1/2 tsp vanilla
1/4 tsp nutmeg
1/2 tsp cinnamon
1 cup sugar
1 cup flour
1 cup milk

Peel and slice potatoes. Place in a medium saucepan with 1/4 cup sugar and with enough water to cover. Bring to boiling, lower heat; cover and cook until potatoes are tender. Set aside.

In a 13x9x2-inch casserole dish, melt butter or margarine in a 350° F oven.
Add potatoes and their cooking juice (up to 2 cups), vanilla and spices.
In a medium bowl, mix sugar, flour and milk.
Pour over potatoes; do not stir.
Return to oven and bake for 45 minutes or until golden brown.

Serves 8 to 10

PEERLESS
SPICES
CINNAMON

FRUIT COBBLER

1 stick butter or margarine
1 can or 1 1/2 cups sweetened fruit
1 cup flour
1 cup sugar
1 cup milk

Melt butter in the bottom of a 13x9x2-inch baking pan.
Pour in fruit, with juices.
In a small mixing bowl, combine flour and sugar, then add milk. Stir
briskly until smooth.
Pour into pan over all. Do not stir.
Bake at 350º F for 30 minutes, or until golden brown on top.

Serves 8

CRANBERRY OATMEAL DELIGHT

16-oz. can whole cranberry sauce
1 1/2 cups cooked apples, chopped
1 cup regular oats, uncooked
1/2 cup firmly packed brown sugar
1/4 cup all-purpose flour
1/4 cup melted butter or margarine
1/2 tsp salt
1/2 cup chopped pecans

In a medium bowl, combine cranberry sauce and apples. Spoon into a buttered 10x6x2-inch baking dish.
In another medium bowl, combine oats, sugar, flour, margarine and salt; spread over cranberry mixture. Sprinkle pecans over top.
Bake at 350º F for 50 minutes or until bubbly. Allow to cool.

Serves 8 to 10

PISTACHIO SALAD

3-oz. pkg. of pistachio pudding mix
1 large container whipped topping
20-oz. can crushed pineapple, undrained
1/2 cup chopped nuts
1 cup miniature marshmallows

In a large bowl, mix pudding mix with whipped topping until blended.
Add pineapple, nuts and marshmallows. Chill for at least 1 hour.

Serves 6 to 8

CHOCOLATE DELIGHT

1 cup flour
1/2 cup margarine, melted
1 cup finely chopped pecans
8-oz. container whipped topping
1 cup powdered sugar
8-oz. pkg. cream cheese
3-oz. pkg. vanilla instant pudding mix
3-oz. pkg. chocolate instant pudding mix
3 cups milk
1/4 cup chopped toasted pecans

In a small bowl, mix flour, margarine and pecans.
Press into a 13x9x2-inch casserole dish.
Bake at 350° F for 20 minutes. Cool.
In a medium size bowl, mix 1 cup whipped topping,
powdered sugar and softened cream cheese until smooth.
Spread over cooled crust. In another medium bowl, mix
both pudding packages with milk according to directions
on box until slightly thickened.
Spread over cream cheese layer. Chill.
Remove from refrigerator and cover with remaining
whipped topping and toasted pecans.
Refrigerate for several hours before serving.

Serves 10 to 12

NOTE: This is without a doubt
everyone's favorite dessert!

189

What could be more convenient than a dessert that is transportable and fits in your hand? Some of the favorites at our house are Peanut Butter Cookies, of course, as well as Brownies, Walnut Drops and Oatmeal Chocolate Chip Cookies. I love Snickerdoodles, because it sounds like a dog's name. I envision an overly pampered, cute little poodle prancing about. But of course the real thing, the cookie, tastes scrumptious. Wrap up some of your favorites with plastic wrap, tie them with ribbon, and place them in one of those colorful biscuit tins, or an antique wooden box to give to a special friend. Or, even better, just grab a handful for yourself and enjoy them before they disappear!

Cookies and Bars

SIX LAYER COOKIE BARS

1 stick margarine
1 cup crushed graham crackers
1 cup coconut
1 cup chocolate chips
1 cup butterscotch chips
8-oz. can Eagle Brand milk
1 cup chopped nuts

Melt margarine in a 13x9x2-inch pan.
Sprinkle crushed graham crackers over melted margarine.
Sprinkle the coconut evenly over cracker crumbs.
Next, layer chocolate chips and butterscotch chips.
Drizzle the Eagle Brand milk (sweetened condensed milk) over all. Top with nuts.
Bake for 30 minutes at 325º F. Cool and cut into bars.

Makes 32 bars

PEANUT BUTTER COOKIES

1 cup shortening
1 cup brown sugar
1 cup white sugar
2 eggs, well beaten
1 cup peanut butter
3 cups plain flour
2 tsp baking soda
1/2 tsp salt

In a large bowl, cream shortening thoroughly. Add sugars gradually.
Add the beaten eggs and peanut butter.
In a medium bowl, sift flour, soda and salt 3 times. Add gradually to
batter; mix well.
Shape into balls the size of walnuts. Place on cookie sheet, 2 inches
apart.
Flatten with a fork in one direction, then in other direction, so fork-
tong pattern crosses.
Bake at 400º F until lightly browned.

Makes 3 to 4 dozen cookies

I Love Peanut Butter!

REFRIGERATOR COOKIES

6 cups sifted all-purpose flour
1/4 tsp salt
1/2 tsp baking soda
1 1/2 cups butter or margarine
1 cup Karo syrup
1/2 cup sugar
1 cup chopped nuts

In a medium bowl, sift together flour, salt and baking soda.
In a large bowl, beat butter until soft and creamy. Add Karo syrup and sugar; beat until thoroughly blended; add nuts. Add sifted dry ingredients all at once; mix thoroughly with hands until stiff dough is formed. Shape into three rolls that are approximately 2 inches in diameter. Wrap in wax paper and chill for 3 to 4 hours in refrigerator. With a very sharp knife, cut into thin slices. Place on an ungreased cookie sheet. Bake at 400° F for 8 to 10 minutes.

Makes about 3 dozen cookies

SNICKERDOODLES

2 tbsp sugar
1 1/2 tsp cinnamon
1 cup margarine, softened
1 1/2 cups sugar
2 eggs
3 cups all-purpose flour
1 1/2 tsp cream of tartar
1 tsp baking soda
Pinch of salt

In a small bowl, combine sugar and cinnamon; set aside.
Preheat oven to 375º F.
In a large bowl, beat together margarine, sugar and
eggs until fluffy.
Add flour, cream of tartar, baking soda and salt; beat
until blended.
Shape into 1-inch balls. Roll in
cinnamon/sugar mixture, coating
completely.
Place 2 1/2 inches apart on ungreased
cookie sheets.
Bake 10 minutes or until golden.
Cool on wire racks.

Makes 3 to 4 dozen

GIANT OATMEAL COOKIES

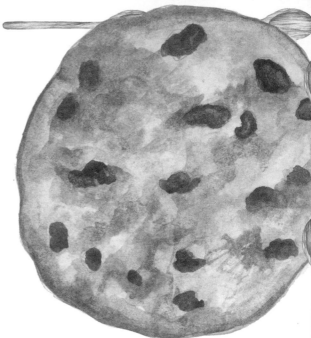

1 1/2 cups all-purpose flour
1/2 tsp baking soda
1/2 tsp salt
2 tsp cinnamon
2 tsp ground cloves
2 tsp ground allspice
1 tsp ground ginger
1 cup butter or margarine, softened
1 cup sugar
1 cup firmly packed brown sugar
2 eggs
1 tsp vanilla
3 cups quick-cooking oats
1 cup chopped nuts (optional)

In medium bowl, combine flour, soda, salt and spices; set aside.
With a mixer, cream butter and sugar in a large bowl. Beat in eggs and vanilla.
Add flour mixture; mix well.
Stir in oats and add nuts.
Drop dough by 1/4-cup measure 5 inches apart on a lightly greased baking sheet.
Bake at 375° F for 12 to 14 minutes or until lightly browned.
Cool slightly on cookie sheet before removing to wire rack to cool completely.

Makes about 2 to 3 dozen cookies

CHOCOLATE CHIP MELTAWAYS

1 cup butter or margarine, softened
1 cup vegetable oil
1 cup sugar
1 cup sifted powdered sugar
2 eggs
4 cups all-purpose flour
1 tsp baking soda
1 tsp cream of tartar
1 tsp salt
1 tsp vanilla
12-oz. pkg. semi-sweet chocolate chips
Additional sugar

In a large bowl, combine butter, oil, sugar, powdered sugar and eggs; beat until smooth.
In a medium bowl, combine flour, soda, cream of tartar and salt. Add to butter mixture; beat until smooth. Stir in vanilla and chocolate chips.
Shape into 1-inch diameter balls and roll in sugar.
Place 2 inches apart on an ungreased cookie sheet.
Bake at 375° F for 10 to 12 minutes or until lightly browned. Cool on wire rack.

Makes approximately 3 dozen cookies

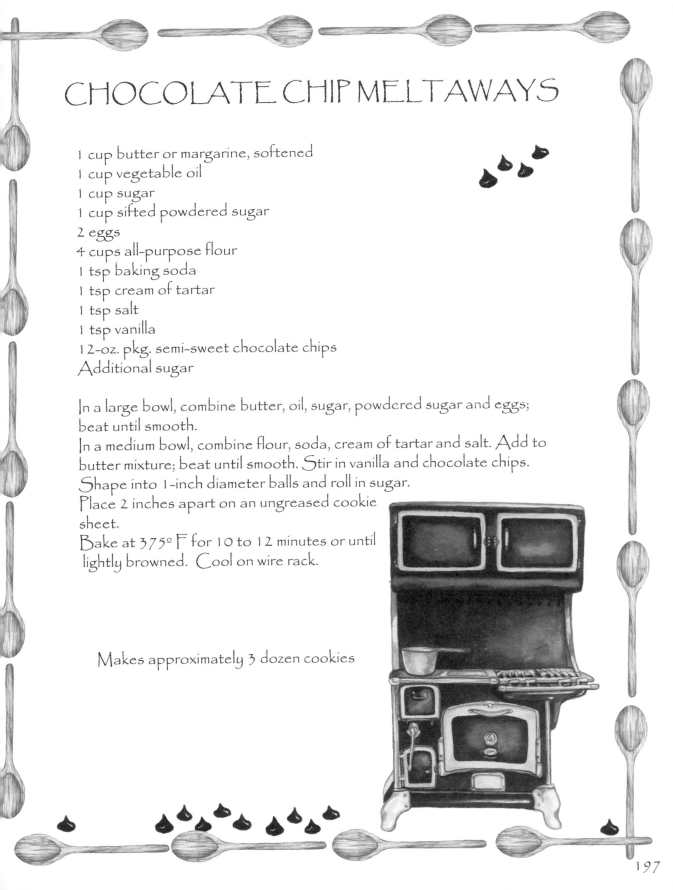

DATE BARS

1/4 cup butter or margarine, softened
3/4 cup sugar
1 egg
1 2/3 cups Bisquick or other biscuit mix
1 cup chopped dates
1/2 cup chopped nuts
3 to 4 tbsp powdered sugar

Preheat oven to 350° F. In a medium bowl, mix butter, sugar and egg until smooth; stir in all remaining ingredients, except powdered sugar.
Spread dough into a greased 8x8x2-inch pan.
Bake for 25 minutes. Cool.
Sprinkle top with powdered sugar. Cut into bars.

Makes 12 bars

EASY BROWNIES

2 cups self-rising flour
2 cups sugar
2 tbsp cocoa
2 sticks margarine, melted
4 eggs
1 tsp vanilla
1 cup chopped pecans

Stir all ingredients together in a large mixing bowl in order listed.
Spread mixture into a greased 8x8x2-inch pan.
Bake at 350° F for 45 minutes. Remove from oven, cool and cut.

Makes 24 brownies

POTATO CANDY

1 potato, peeled and cooked
Sifted powdered sugar
Peanut butter

While potato is still warm, mash thoroughly. Add enough powdered
sugar to make a stiff consistency, stiff enough to roll out
with a rolling pin. Roll out onto a flat surface.
Spread enough peanut butter to cover.
Roll up jellyroll-fashion and slice into 1/4-inch
pieces.

Makes about 36 pieces of candy

OATMEAL CHOCOLATE CHIP COOKIES

1 cup shortening
3/4 cup sugar
3/4 cup brown sugar
2 eggs
1 tsp vanilla
1 1/2 cups flour
1/4 cup cocoa
1 tsp salt
1 tsp baking soda
1 tsp hot water
2 cups oats
1 cup chopped nuts
12 oz. semi-sweet chocolate chips

In a large mixing bowl, cream shortening and sugars. Add eggs and vanilla; beat well.
Add flour, cocoa, salt and soda; mix until blended.
Stir in hot water, oats, nuts and chocolate chips.
Drop dough, by rounded teaspoonfuls, 1 inch apart onto greased cookie sheets. Bake at 350° F for 10 to 12 minutes.

Makes 4 to 5 dozen cookies

LEMON PIE BARS

1 cup butter
2 cups flour
1/2 cup powdered sugar
4 eggs
1 tbsp grated lemon peel
1/4 cup flour
1/4 cup lemon juice
2 cups sugar
1 tsp baking powder

In a large bowl, combine butter, 2 cups flour and powdered sugar to make pie crust and pat evenly into a 13x9x2-inch pan. Bake for 20 minutes at 350º F. Remove from oven; cool.
In a medium bowl, combine eggs, lemon peel, 1/4 cup flour, lemon juice, sugar and baking powder; mix well.
Pour over the baked crust and bake 25 minutes more. Let cool, then cover with icing.

ICING
1 1/2 cups powdered sugar
2 tbsp lemon juice

Blend in a small bowl. Spread over bars.

Makes 24 bars

WALNUT DROPS

2 cups all-purpose flour
1 tsp baking soda
Dash salt
1/2 cup shortening
1/3 cup butter or margarine
1/4 cup confectioners' sugar
2 tbsp heavy cream
1 tsp vanilla
2 cups coarsely chopped walnuts

Preheat oven to 325º F and grease 2 cookie
sheets.
In a large bowl, sift together flour, baking soda
and salt; set aside.
In a medium bowl, mix shortening and butter
together until soft. Add sugar gradually;
mix until creamy. Add cream and vanilla.
Stir in flour mixture. Add nuts and mix in well.
Roll dough into 1-inch balls and place 1 inch
apart on a baking sheet.
Bake for 30 minutes. Remove to baking rack to
cool.
When cool, roll balls in confectioners' sugar to
coat.

Makes about 3 dozen drops

MOON PIES

1/2 cup butter or margarine, softened
1 cup sugar
1 egg
1 cup evaporated milk
1 tsp vanilla extract
2 cups all-purpose flour
1/2 tsp salt
1/2 cup unsweetened cocoa
1 1/2 tsp baking soda
1/2 tsp baking powder
1/2 cup butter or margarine, softened
1 cup confectioners' sugar
1/2 tsp vanilla extract
1 cup marshmallow cream

Preheat over to 400° F. Lightly grease a cookie sheet.
To make cookie crusts: In a large mixing bowl, créme together 1/2 cup butter or margarine and sugar. Add egg, evaporated milk and vanilla; mix well.
In a separate bowl, mix together flour, salt, cocoa, baking soda and baking powder. Add flour mixture slowly to the sugar mixture while stirring. Mix until all ingredients are combined.
Drop the dough onto the greased cookie sheet by rounded tablespoons. Leave at least 3 inches between cookies as dough will spread as it bakes.
Bake in preheated oven for 6 to 8 minutes, or until firm when pressed with fingertip. Allow to cool at least one hour.
To make marshmallow filling: In a medium mixing bowl, blend together 1/2 cup butter or margarine, confectioners' sugar and marshmallow cream; mix until smooth.
Assemble pies by spreading 1 to 2 tbsp of filling on the flat side of a cookie crust, and then cover with another cookie.

Makes 2 dozen pies

We love smoothies. And we tend to invent a different one every time we take out the blender because the ingredients are ever-changing. At our house, you could close the refrigerator fully stocked at night, and open it the next morning to find half the ingredients gone -- ERS: empty refrigerator syndrome. So, you learn to adjust a recipe accordingly.

Peanut Butter and Jelly Smoothies may sound weird, but they are delicious, trust me. Southern Sweet Tea is included here so that hopefully anyone from north of the Mason-Dixon Line can learn to make it correctly. End of the Day Cosmo is sometimes my answer to the strains and stresses of a long, busy day. I tend to make mine to my own taste, which includes very little cranberry juice. It turns out a soft baby pink, and has the kick of a mule. And, as a rule, there is no orange peel or cherry in mine, due to, you guessed it, ERS.

Beverages

ORANGE BLOSSOM PUNCH

6 6-oz. cans frozen orange juice concentrate, thawed, undiluted
9 cups water
3 12-oz. cans apricot nectar, chilled
3 12-oz. bottles ginger ale, chilled
Ice

Combine orange juice concentrate and water in a punch bowl; mix well.
Pour in apricot nectar and ginger ale; mix and add ice.

Serves 24

BANANA STRAWBERRY SMOOTHIE

2 1/2 cups ice
1 cup fresh strawberries, stems removed
1 large banana
1/2 cup fat-free half-and-half
1/2 cup sugar

Place all ingredients in a blender. Purée on high for 1 minute. Stir, and purée again until ingredients are blended, thick and smooth. Serve in tall glasses with a straw.

Makes 3 drinks

PEANUT BUTTER AND JELLY SMOOTHIE

2 1/2 cups ice
1 cup strawberries, stems removed
1/4 cup strawberry juice, or strawberry/pineapple juice
1/3 cup fat-free half-and-half
3 tbsp peanut butter
1/4 cup sugar

Place all ingredients in a blender. Purée until ice begins to crush. Stop, stir and repeat until all ingredients are blended and consistency is thick and smooth.
Serve in a tall glass with a straw.

Makes 3 drinks

TROPICAL SMOOTHIE

2 1/2 cups ice
1/2 cup juice (orange or pineapple)
1/3 cup pineapple chunks
1 whole banana, peeled
1 whole mango (fruit only)
1/4 cup sugar

Place all ingredients in a blender. Purée on high for 1 minute.
Stop, stir, and blend again until all ingredients are blended.
Consistency should be thick and smooth.
Pour into tall glasses; serve with straws.

Makes 3 drinks

NOTE: Coconut rum may also be added for an alcoholic version.

RUSSIAN TEA

1 quart water
12 whole cloves
Juice of 2 lemons plus rinds
Juice of 3 oranges plus rinds
2 quarts sweetened tea (see Southern Sweet Tea)

In a large saucepan, add water and cloves bound in a piece of cheesecloth; heat to boiling. Peel the rinds from the lemons and oranges and add to the saucepan; boil for 5 minutes. Remove bag of cloves and rinds.
Add sweetened tea and the lemon and orange juices. Serve hot.

Makes 12 to 16 servings

INSTANT RUSSIAN TEA

3 cups sugar
1/2 cup instant tea mix
1/2 tsp cinnamon
1/2 tsp allspice
2 cups Tang orange drink

Mix together and store in a jar until ready for use.
Add 1 tsp (or more to make stronger) to 1 cup hot water.

NOTE: This makes a great holiday gift in a pretty jar tied with a ribbon. Tie a tag on it with instructions.

Aprox. 30 cups

SOUTHERN SWEET TEA

3 family-size tea bags (I like Luzianne)
Water
1 cup sugar

The old-fashioned way: In a medium saucepan, heat 2 quarts of water to boiling.
Drop in tea bags. Remove from heat and allow to steep for about 5 minutes.
Add sugar and stir until dissolved. Using a funnel, pour into a gallon-size container (we use a milk jug, washed of course). Fill the rest of the way with cool, clear water.
Screw on lid and shake until blended. Enjoy over a large glass with ice.

Makes 1 gallon

We now use a Mr. Coffee Iced Tea Maker, which is much simpler.
The ingredients are the same, but the method varies somewhat.
Fill provided pitcher with cold water. Pour as much as will fit into the brewer.
Place tea bags in the holder for tea. Push on button. When all the water has brewed through, add the sugar and stir. Serve over ice.

WEDDING PUNCH

2 46-oz. cans red Hawaiian punch, chilled
1 quart apple juice, chilled
2-liter bottle ginger ale

Mix together punch and apple juice.
Add ginger ale just before serving.

Serves 24 to 30

LEMONADE

1 3/4 cups white sugar
8 cups water
3 lemons
1 1/2 cups fresh lemon juice
Lemon slices

In a small saucepan, combine sugar and 1 cup water.
Bring to boiling and stir until sugar is dissolved. Allow to
cool to room temperature.
Cover and refrigerate until chilled.
Juice lemons and remove seeds, but leave pulp. In a large
pitcher, stir together the chilled syrup, lemon juice and the remaining
7 cups of water.
Serve with fresh lemon slices over ice.

Makes 8 servings

STRAWBERRY PUNCH

10-oz. package frozen strawberries in syrup
2 6-oz. cans frozen orange juice concentrate
1 can frozen lemonade concentrate
6 cups cold water
2 1/2 cups chilled ginger ale

Thaw strawberries. Combine concentrates and water;
chill. Pour into punch bowl and add ginger ale and
strawberries.

Makes 24 servings

KISSES HOT CHOCOLATE

1 cup fat-free half-and-half for each cup of chocolate
5 Hershey's Kisses for each cup
Whipped cream, if desired

In a medium saucepan, pour in half-and-half. Warm to steaming, but not boiling. Into each cup, place 5 Kisses. Pour in hot half-and-half and stir until dissolved. Add whipped cream on top, if desired.

COZY HOT CHOCOLATE

2 tbsp baking cocoa
2 tbsp sugar
1/4 cup water
2 cups milk

1/2 tsp vanilla
Whipped cream
Cinnamon

In a medium saucepan, mix the cocoa and sugar and add water. Bring to a boil, stirring constantly; boil for 1 minute. Reduce heat, add milk and heat through. Remove from heat and stir in vanilla. Pour into two cups; top with whipped cream and sprinkle with cinnamon or cocoa, if desired.

Makes 2 servings

LATTE

1/2 cup fat-free half-and-half
1/2 cup strong fresh coffee, flavored or Colombian
Sugar to taste

Pour half-and-half into a microwave-safe cup. Heat for
30 seconds on high, or until steaming.
Add coffee to fill cup to top and stir in sugar to your
taste.

Makes 1 serving

IRISH COFFEE

1 3/4 oz. Irish whiskey
2 tsp brown sugar
3 1/2 oz. hot coffee
2 tbsp whipped cream

Pour the whiskey into a clear-glass coffee mug with a handle (actually,
any kind of cup will work, but these look especially nice and authentic);
add the sugar and stir.
Add the hot coffee and stir.
Gently spoon whipped cream onto the top;
do not stir.

Makes 1 serving

SANGRIA PUNCH
(no alchohol)

3/4 cup lemonade mix (I prefer Country Time brand.)
4 cups cranberry juice cocktail
1 cup orange juice
1 tbsp fresh lime juice
3 cups club soda
2 medium oranges, sliced
2 medium limes, sliced

In a large pitcher, pour drink mix, juices and stir until lemonade mix is dissolved. Chill. Just before serving, add the club soda and fruit. Serve over ice.

Makes 8 servings

SIDECAR

1 oz. brandy
2/3 oz. Cointreau
2/3 oz. fresh lemon juice

Pour ingredients into a shaker filled with ice. Shake vigorously. Strain into a martini glass.

Makes 1 drink

Yeah, I know it's not a sidecar, it's a pedal car...

APRICOT BELLINIS

6 fresh apricots, halved (about 1/2 pound)
1 11-oz. can apricot nectar
1/4 cup sugar
1 1/2 cups champagne
Crushed ice
Garnishes: fresh apricot slices, fresh mint sprigs

Process first 3 ingredients in a blender until smooth, stopping to scrape down sides. Stir in champagne, and serve immediately over crushed ice. Garnish, if desired.

Makes 4 drinks

BLUE MOON

1 oz. vodka
1 oz. blue Curaçao
Dash of lemonade

Fill a martini glass with ice and water and set aside to chill.
Fill a cocktail shaker with ice, lots of ice. Add vodka, blue Curaçao and a bit of lemonade. Shake until totally chilled.
Empty water and ice from glass. Strain drink into the martini glass.

Makes 1 drink

When I make them they are the color of a swimming pool; perfect!

END of the DAY COSMO

1 3/4 oz. vodka (Ketel One is my favorite brand)
1/3 oz. Cointreau or Triple Sec
1/3 oz. cranberry juice
1/3 oz. fresh lime juice
Orange peel slice or cherry for garnish

Hide the telephone in the sofa cushions, put out the dog and lock the front door.
Fill a martini glass with ice and water to chill.
Fill cocktail shaker with ice, lots of ice. Add all ingredients and shake until your hand is freezing.
Pour out the ice water from the martini glass and immediately strain mixer contents into the glass. Trace around the edge of the glass with the orange peel. Then drop it in. Some like to use a cherry, suit yourself. Sit back in a private place and enjoy.

Makes 1 drink

INDEX

Rice Pudding 184
Wild Rice Salad 55
Rice Pudding 184
Romano Shrimp-stuffed Mushrooms 9
Russian Tea 208
Salads
Avocado Salad 51
Avocado, Tomato and Fresh Mozzarella Salad 60
Blueberry Salad 62
Copper Pennies 58
English Pea Salad 57
Hawaiian Rice Salad 61
Macaroni Salad 53
Pasta Salad with Garlic Mayo 59
Seven Layer Salad 50
Seven-cup Salad 57
Southern Bean Salad 54
Summer Squash Salad 52
Three Bean Salad 56
Watermelon Salad 63
Wild Rice Salad 55
Salmon-stuffed Tomatoes 130
Sandwiches
California Pita 85
Egg Salad Sandwiches 80
Goat Cheese and Salmon Sandwiches 87
Grilled Cuban Sandwiches 83
Open-faced Monte Cristo 86
Open-faced Roast Beef Sandwiches 84
Open-faced Turkey Sandwich with Apple 81
Peanut Butter, Apple and Bacon Sandwich 82
Turkey Pita 85
Sangria Punch 213
Sausages
Galumpous 111
Pigs in a Blanket 11
Sausage and Cheese Balls 20
Sausage and Onion Bake 118
Sausage Gravy 116
Sausage and Cheese Balls 20
Sausage and Onion Bake 118

Sausage Gravy 116
Seven Layer Salad 50
Seven-cup Salad 57
Shepherd's Pie 107
Shrimp
Baked Tilapia with Shrimp Sauce 127
Crab and Shrimp Casserole 128
Curried Shrimp 122
Mushroom Shrimp Creole 123
Romano Shrimp-stuffed Mushrooms 9
Spinach and Mushroom Stew with Shrimp 43
Sidecar 213
Side Dishes
Bethany's Baked Beans 68
Broccoli and Rice Casserole 68
Broccoli Casserole 76
Butternut Squash Casserole 70
Candied Carrots 71
Coleslaw 71
Corn Casserole 74
Creole Cabbage 73
Green Bean Casserole 75
Hash Brown Potato Casserole 69
Honey-baked Onions 77
Mashed Potatoes 72
Squash-Carrot Casserole 66
Sweet Potato Soufflé 67
Six Layer Cookie Bars 192
Smoked Salmon Spaghetti 136
Snickerdoodles 195
Soups
Cauliflower Chowder 41
Chicken and Potato Soup 39
Creamy Potato Soup 44
Easy Chicken and Dumplings 42
French Onion Soup 46
Homemade Chicken Noodle Soup 45
Red Pepper and Fish Soup 37
Spinach and Mushroom Stew with Shrimp 43
Taco Soup 40
Tomato Basil Soup 47

Notes